Becoming
Holy
Women

Becoming Holy Women

MARCIA L. MITCHELL

BEACON HILL PRESS OF KANSAS CITY
KANSAS CITY, MISSOURI

ISBN: 083-411-4224

Printed in the
United States of America

Cover Design: Crandall Vail

10 9 8 7 6 5 4 3 2 1

To my mother
Dorothy M. Hein

Thank you for your many prayers.
I love you.

Contents

Preface

Writing about holiness has been quite a challenge for me. It's not that I have arrived, and now I'm telling others how to be as holy as I am. Rather, I've found the path marked "holiness unto the Lord," and I'd like others to walk that path along with me.

As I have read and studied much of what our forefathers have written on holiness, I have learned that it can be a difficult subject. In my reading, I found apparent contradictions. Sometimes the language was so archaic the meaning was obscured. Occasionally the writing was pretty dull. Yet the message was beautiful, refreshing, and full of life.

This vibrancy of living the Christian life to its fullest was exactly what I needed, and I wanted to share it with others. Some of the people I know won't make the effort or take the time to wade through those dusty old tomes, but they need to hear the message. So I've attempted in these pages to make the message more palatable. The first two chapters are strong ones and may be a bit difficult at first. Yet, I challenge you to read them. Take the time to learn about the message of holiness.

The rest of the book is a look at contemporary Christianity and how we can live the life of holiness today. Holiness is not just a moment of infilling power of the Holy Spirit, but it is also very practical and ongoing. The Holy Spirit lives with us daily, helping us work out in our lives the holiness that is within us.

May God bless you as you start on this challenging, practical, and exciting venture in your Christian walk.

1

What Is Holiness?

*"I just can't be as holy as ... say, a preacher or a missionary."
Molly shrugged her shoulders. "It doesn't seem necessary to me. Be-
sides, God understands me. All I need is enough religion to get me
into heaven." She shoved away from the table, nearly spilling her
half-empty coffee cup. "Why should women have to become holy,
anyway? These aren't Bible times. In today's modern world women
just don't have time to sit around and be holy!"*

Becoming holy women is not getting by with as little
of God in your life as you can, but going all the way—becoming all you can for God! It isn't toe-dipping religion, but
taking a headlong plunge. It's soaking up all of God we can
and asking for more.

That half-empty coffee cup is symbolic of Molly's spiritual life. God offered her a full cup of himself, but she chose
to accept just enough to save her "skin." Religion, for some,
is only skin deep. They value what shows on the outside,
but deep inside they still want total control, excluding God.

The Bible says God wants the whole person, not just the
outside.

> Therefore, I urge you, brothers, in view of God's
> mercy, to offer your bodies as living sacrifices, holy and
> pleasing to God—this is your spiritual act of worship.
> Do not conform any longer to the pattern of this world,
> but be transformed by the renewing of your mind. Then
> you will be able to test and approve what God's will is—
> his good, pleasing and perfect will *(Rom. 12:1-2).*

The challenge of the holy life, then, is how much we can become like Christ. We want the whole cup of righteousness that God has served us. We don't want to be deceived or cheated out of the full blessing God wants to give.

Holiness is the growing edge of our spiritual life; come and grow with me through these chapters. Let us be transformed by renewing our minds—studying Scripture and applying it to our lives. Let's begin today the process of **becoming holy women.**

"I just can't be perfect!" Edith sat in a chair across from me, her cup full of tea still untouched and cooling.

"I became a Christian seven years ago." She twisted the cup nervously. "But to be absolutely honest, there are times when it hasn't been that great. I mean—I love God, and I love Jesus, and I'm grateful for salvation, but sometimes I struggle so hard to do what I think is right, and then I fall flat on my face and blow the whole thing!"

She shook her head sadly. "I don't think it's possible 100 percent of the time to be the holy person the Bible portrays."

Edith is right in one way—she can't be perfect, at least not the way she sees it. She is *struggling* to be perfect—and that's the problem. Not one of us has the ability within ourselves to accomplish perfection, human or otherwise.

The apostle Paul experienced the same type of struggle trying to do what is good and ending up doing just the opposite:

> For I have the desire to do what is good, but I cannot carry it out. For what I do is not the good I want to do; no, the evil I do not want to do—this I keep on doing *(Rom. 7:18-19).*

If we can't do the good we would like to do, what then is the purpose in becoming a Christian? Is it just to make it to heaven somehow? Do we ask forgiveness for our sins and then place a check mark by that item? "Well, I did that," we might say, "and now I can live my life and wait until I die, knowing I'll go to heaven."

Or is there something else, something more we are supposed to do between accepting Christ as our Savior and walking through the pearly gates?

> But just as he who called you is holy, so be holy in
> all you do; for it is written: "Be holy, because I am holy"
> *(1 Pet. 1:15-16).*

If God is holy and He has said we are to also be holy, then how holy is God? Are there degrees of holiness like rungs on a ladder that must be taken step by step? If so, how is it possible to move up on the ladder marked "Holy"? Can we live a holy life today? It seems impossible, yet the Bible says we're supposed to do it. Isn't that verse outdated? Maybe it needs to be reevaluated in light of today's society. God really doesn't expect us to be holy, not today—or does He?

The meaning of "holy" is found in the person of God, the most holy or most sacred One; the absolute Holy One in His purity, majesty, and glory. There isn't anyone or anything more sacred or more holy than God. He is absolutely pure.

Pure. That's how holy God is.

Pure. That's how holy He commands us to be.

Recently, I sat on my patio playing with my neighbor's kitten. She slipped down from my lap and crouched attentively, watching a butterfly dancing in the afternoon sun. As the butterfly dipped and flitted, the kitten would leap and spin, trying to match its movements. But no matter how hard the kitten tried, she couldn't get high enough. In a few minutes the butterfly caught a passing breeze and fluttered out of sight.

The only way that kitten could have hoped to match the butterfly was to become a butterfly. The differences between them were too great. The only thing a kitten can become is a cat. It cannot create wings in place of paws.

We can try with all our might, all our power, all our concentration to be as holy as God is. But at the very best we can produce only an imitation. We can refrain from a sinful life; we can read our Bibles and go to church; we can do good to others—but it still isn't the holiness of God.

We can imitate the life of Christ to the best of our ability, but it will be a poor shadow of the purity and holiness that God has commanded. There is, however, one thing that will change our efforts from being an imitation into the real holiness of God's command.

In His high-priestly prayer, Jesus had one major focus as He prayed for His disciples and for all of us who would become His followers.

> I pray . . . that all of them may be one, Father, just as you are in me and I am in you. May they also be in us (*John 17:20-21*).

Jesus prayed that we would become **one** with himself and the Father. This was to be accomplished by allowing the Father to indwell the disciple in the same manner that the Father indwelt the Son and by the disciple remaining in the Father just as the Son was one with the Father. (See also John 10:30, 38; 14:10; and 17:11.)

The apostle Paul said:

> In him the whole building is joined together and rises to become a holy temple in the Lord. And in him you too are being built together to become a dwelling in which God lives by his Spirit (*Eph. 2:21-22*).

It is the Holy Spirit of God by His indwelling of us that causes us to become one with the Father and with Christ. This is the only way we can fulfill God's command to be holy even as He is holy.

 We are not to imitate the holiness of God but are to allow *Christ to be holy in us.* His indwelling creates the holiness God commands, changing our imitation into the real thing.

Jesus knew we couldn't become holy through our own efforts. As He neared the moment of the Cross, He offered hope to the disciples.

> Now I am going to him who sent me . . . But I tell
> you the truth: It is for your good that I am going away.
> Unless I go away, the Counselor will not come to you;
> but if I go, I will send him to you *(John 16:5, 7).*

Jesus knew the disciples would need guidance when they couldn't ask Him face-to-face how to handle a situation. They would need an instant replay when they couldn't ask Him to repeat a lesson or truth He had taught them. Who would keep them on the path of righteousness when He was no longer there?

God the Father and God the Son together were going to send God the Holy Spirit (the Comforter), who could do all those things. Jesus called Him the *Paraklētos.* This Greek word means *one who is called alongside to comfort and to give aid.* The disciples were going to need help, and in God's great plan, the Comforter would provide that help.

The last hours before the Cross, Jesus taught the disciples explicit truths about the Holy Spirit. This was the most important information they would need. And if it was that important to the disciples, then it's of importance to us.

As soon as He mentioned the Comforter, Jesus listed the type of work the Holy Spirit would do. In addition to comforting the disciples, His job would be to "convict the world of guilt" in three major areas: "sin and righteousness and judgment" (John 16:8).

Jesus knew the disciples could not attain God's required righteousness through their own efforts. They needed the Holy Spirit, God himself, to produce godlikeness in their hearts.

But what are the conditions for holiness? In fact, what exactly is holiness?

From the time we are old enough to know the difference between right and wrong, we deliberately choose to do one or the other. It is a matter of our will. You can either *will* to do right, or you can *will* to do wrong. When you *will* to do wrong, it is a conscious choice against God because you *know* what is right. That is known as willful sin, sins we commit for which we are responsible. This is one of two sin problems that must be acknowledged and dealt with. We need to seek God's forgiveness for willful sin.

Beyond willful sin, there is a sinful nature within each of us for which we are not responsible. Yet this, too, needs to be confronted and yielded to God.

It is this inborn sinful nature or "original sin" that Paul talks about when he said,

> I have the desire to do what is good, but I cannot carry it out *(Rom. 7:18)*.

The apostle Paul, one of the greatest examples of a person who has been converted, freely admits there is still a sinful nature within himself that needs divine help.

Does this mean God expects us to continue sinning after we have sought His forgiveness? Absolutely not! The Bible clearly says,

> No one who is born of God will continue to sin, because God's seed remains in him; he cannot go on sinning, because he has been born of God *(1 John 3:9)*.

If God doesn't expect us to continue sinning, yet this original sin remains within us, what *does* God expect?

Over and over the Bible declares that God expects us to be pure and holy:

> Blessed are the pure in heart, for they will see God *(Matt. 5:8)*.

> Make every effort to live in peace with all men and to be holy; without holiness no one will see the Lord *(Heb. 12:14)*.

> For it is written: "Be holy, because I am holy" *(1 Pet. 1:16)*.

What kind of people ought you to be? You ought to
live holy and godly lives *(2 Pet. 3:11)*.

When the apostle Peter was making his report about
the Gentiles to the other disciples at Jerusalem, he described
the purification process like this:

God, who knows the heart, showed that he accepted
them by giving the Holy Spirit to them, just as he did to
us. He made no distinction between us and them, for he
purified their hearts by faith *(Acts 15:8-9)*.

As clearly as possible, Peter says their hearts were purified in a twofold act.

1. The people expressed their *faith*.
2. God gave the *Holy Spirit*.

This is a covenant between God and man, each ful-
filling a specific part. The result is that man's heart, through
faith, is purified by the Holy Spirit, God's Gift. Our faith
makes this possible—and results in a condition of heart
(pureness) that is satisfactory to God, that fulfills His re-
quirements.

The two acts of God (forgiveness and purification) are
stated again in Titus 2:13-14:

Jesus Christ, who gave himself for us to redeem us
from all wickedness and to purify for himself a people
that are his very own, eager to do what is good.

Just as we are taught to *ask for forgiveness*, so we are told
to *ask for the Holy Spirit*.

If you then, though you are evil, know how to give
good gifts to your children, how much more will your
Father in heaven give the Holy Spirit to those who ask
him! *(Luke 11:13)*.

This condition of holiness is available to us through
prayer. Ask God for it and He will respond. But when He
does respond, is it an immediate change or is it a lifelong
growing process?

Phoebe Palmer is sometimes referred to as the "mother

of the Holiness Revival." She and her husband, Dr. Walter C. Palmer, began in the 1840s to spread the teaching of holiness throughout the Northeast. Her main message, whether spoken or written in her books and magazine, was "Holiness . . . *now.*" Immediacy was emphasized both on the part of the seeker and on the part of God. Come to God *now,* she insisted, and when the conditions for holiness are met, God will fulfill His promise of holiness *now.* [1]

When we seek holiness in our Christian walk, there is a moment when it begins. There is an immediate response from God through the gift of His Holy Spirit. But there is also a process of growth, a continuing path of learning how to apply and become the holy person God expects.

First, we become aware that there is something lacking in our Christian walk. We will sense God showing us that our hearts have a tendency to prefer *self* over what He wants.

Bowing before God, who has forgiven our sins, we now surrender the preference of *self.* We are not letting go of who we are, because our personality and individuality are retained. Rather, we are yielding our "self rights" to God.

God will be examining heart motives at this point. It won't do to just parrot the words. He wants to know if we really want to be holy so much that we are willing to be changed by Him.

Are we willing to commit ourselves to God in total obedience? This step is a deliberate decision on each person's part. Each of us must know exactly what we are doing. We are consecrating our whole life to do whatever He wants, whenever He wants us to do it, however He asks us to perform the tasks.

When these questions are answered with a resounding "YES," God will immediately respond to our act of faith in asking for the Holy Spirit. God will not withhold any good gift from us. Our faith is the key that opens our hearts to receiving the Holy Spirit.

He redeemed us in order that the blessing given to Abraham might come to the Gentiles through Christ Jesus, so that by faith we might receive the promise of the Spirit *(Gal. 3:14)*.

For the disciples (Acts 2:2) and the people in the house of Cornelius (10:44) there was a specific moment in time when God poured out His Holy Spirit. It was an immediate act, a crisis moment in each person's spiritual life. One minute they were seeking a change in their heart, waiting for God's promise, and the next moment God acted, pouring himself into their hearts.

Crisis experience? Yes. An end beyond which no one can go in their spiritual growth? No.

The purity of heart that God gives us in a moment is different from maturity of character. Just as it takes years for even God to grow a tree, so maturity in Christ is the result of growing in His grace. Maturity does not happen instantaneously or automatically.

On a cold winter afternoon, I thumbed through a bright seed and plant catalog, feasting my eyes on sun-drenched scenes of yards filled with fruit trees and gorgeous flowers. There is a clear psychological reason the merchants mail those catalogs in the dead of winter! In moments I had filled out the order blank, including an order for two miniature fruit trees, the kind that "produce edible fruit right in your living room!" Eventually spring arrived, and so did my order. The two fruit trees were included just as they promised, but they were far from those depicted in the glorious ads.

Two scrawny wisps of green mocked me day after day as I faithfully tended their bare limbs and scraggled roots. Two long years later they were healthy enough to sit on my back porch. One July afternoon the temperature suddenly soared, bursting the 105-degree mark. In the busyness of summer, I forgot my plants until a few days later, when I noticed the leaves dropping violently from one of the tiny trees. In my neglect, one tree had become sunburned beyond rescue and had to be discarded.

With renewed vigor I turned my attention to the remaining tree. I checked it daily, watched for bugs and blight, pruned and groomed it, and monitored temperature and sunlight. Finally, four years later the dream has come true. It's almost Christmas, and there are two bulging, thumb-sized oranges and three beautiful white blossoms on my miniature tree to help chase away winter's gloom.

There should have been *two* trees! Neglect exacted a heavy price.

Any seed, given the right conditions, can sprout and even grow. But it needs careful nurturing to turn it into a beautiful, fruitful, mature plant. Neglected, it may become twisted, stunted, diseased, or it may even die.

This same type of careful attention needs to be given to the holy life within us. Neglect will also take its toll in our relationship with Christ. We must make a conscious choice to become Christlike and holy in His sight.

The apostle Paul said:

> Not that I have already obtained all this, or have already been made perfect, but I press on to take hold of that for which Christ Jesus took hold of me *(Phil. 3:12)*.

We are to "press on" in the process of perfection. In this sense, we can never get to a point where we can smugly say, "I do not need to go beyond this point. I can sit here and rest, knowing I am perfect." In every area of our lives, there are always things, whether large or small, that need faithful nurturing. If we are not growing, we are decaying.

This holiness, sometimes called "sanctification," is a continuing process. Although we consciously work toward the goal of Christlikeness, it is actually created in us through the power of the Holy Spirit.

> And we . . . are being transformed into his likeness
> with ever-increasing glory, which comes from the Lord,
> who is the Spirit *(2 Cor. 3:18).*

Once holiness happens in our hearts, the work isn't finished. There is always the potential danger of carelessness.
At any point in our lives there can be a slow return to sinning through neglect. We will always need to be alert to af-
flictions that can attack the life of holiness.

Holiness isn't a state of being pure and petrified. We
aren't carved in stone, polished and immobile. Holiness is
alive. It blossoms and grows as we nurture it. But there is
never a time in our lives where sin becomes an impossibil-
ity. We are never immune from temptation or susceptibility
to sin. Through negligence and lack of watchfulness, sin can
become once again part of our lives. God will not force us to
be holy. The choice is always ours.

> My dear children, I write this to you so that you
> will not sin. But if anybody does sin, we have one who
> speaks to the Father in our defense—Jesus Christ, the
> Righteous One *(1 John 2:1).*

The first part of that verse says, "so that you *will* not
sin" (italics mine). We don't have to sin; we have a choice.
It's a choice each of us must exercise constantly as the Holy
Spirit lives and breathes within us, whispering His guidance for our everyday lives. The possibility to sin is there,
but we don't have to give in to it.

As we consistently walk in holiness, we will become
sensitive to the possibility of sin. Things that may seem un-
important to other people will become vastly significant to
our spiritual life and growth. However, when we fail to
heed the warnings and sin as a result, it is extremely important to remember that we have an advocate, "one who
speaks to the Father in our defense." When John wrote that
letter, he understood well that we would need encouragement when we failed God. He also wrote:

> If we confess our sins, he is faithful and just and
> will forgive us our sins and purify us from all un-
> righteousness *(1 John 1:9).*

This verse tells us that Jesus is there to defend us and to
forgive us when we confess and return to the Father.

There is something else that holiness isn't. It isn't, and
never can be, absolute perfection. Holiness does not produce
perfect humans who cannot sin or make a mistake. The
apostle Paul wrote to the Christians in the Philippian
church to urge them to keep on growing. He didn't want
them to think he (or they) had "arrived" and could rest on
their past. Read his words:

> Brothers, I do not consider myself yet to have taken
> hold of it. But one thing I do: Forgetting what is behind
> and straining toward what is ahead, I press on toward
> the goal to win the prize for which God has called me
> heavenward in Christ Jesus *(3:13-14).*

God doesn't want us posed and petrified; He wants us
pliable and growing. In his book *My Utmost for His Highest,*
Oswald Chambers said that we are not called to produce ad-
miration for ourselves but are to live a life in such perfect
relationship to God that it produces a longing for God in
the hearts of others.[2]

Because we are not perfect humans, we can make mistakes in judgment. Because holiness does not give us perfect
knowledge, we may form erroneous opinions that lead to
false judgments.

John Wesley, well-known proponent of the holiness
movement in the 1700s, never used the term *sinless perfection.*
Instead, he pointed out that Christian perfection is loving
God with all the heart, soul, mind, and strength, and one's
neighbor as oneself. This perfection does not present any
conflicts. It is possible to love God with all you have and
are, including loving your neighbor as much as you love
yourself, and still lack good judgment.

Perfection, then, is our relationship with God in love and obedience. We are faulty humans living in a fractured world, but our relationship with God can still be whole and perfect. Holiness is an inner perfection.

* * *

THINK ON THESE THINGS

1. Do you want to move beyond the constant struggle of knowing what is right to do in God's sight, yet feeling unable to become the holy person God expects?

2. Are you imitating Christ's life or are you alive in Christ? How can you know the difference?

3. What "corners of your life" are you withholding from Jesus? Pray about yielding them.

4. Having been filled with God's Holy Spirit, is it possible to "lose" this state of holiness? If so, what exactly would bring about this change?

5. If you have sinned, what can you do to restore a right relationship with God?

6. What mistakes in judgment have you made that you thought were sin? Take time right now to bring these matters to God in prayer and allow Him to put them into proper perspective in your life.

7. As you are growing and maturing in holiness, what specific areas in your life need some renewed attention and nurturing?

* * *

Books to read:

Sanctification in the New Testament, Ralph Earle
Grace, Faith, and Holiness, H. Ray Dunning
The Way of Holiness, Phoebe Palmer
The Fullness of the Spirit, William M. Greathouse

2

The Path of Holiness

"I don't think holiness fits in today's world." Janice shook her head. "It's like wearing a white satin dress to muck out the stable!" She covered her cup of tea protectively with her hands. "If we're going to survive in our society today, we have to fit in with our surroundings. God knows what's in my heart and how much I love Him. He understands there are certain things I have to do to get along in my everyday world, even if they don't fit with these standards of holiness."

Janice is right about our contemporary culture. It certainly doesn't line up with heart holiness! But Janice is clearly wrong when it comes to how we should live in today's society. We need to establish our focal point. Which one is out of step, holiness or today's culture?

For the Christian, holiness is the normal way of life. To line yourself up with Christ makes the world out of step. If we line up with the world, then holiness doesn't fit. We need to choose our point of view.

Does the holiness God wants change with society? In my growing-up years, I met a lady with her hair knotted on top of her head, no makeup, and a black dress with a white collar. She said she dressed that way because she was a Christian. I thought she must be a very holy person to be willing to look so out of place. I also thought, looking at her, that the Bible required women to look and dress like that.

I am not belittling this woman. It was important to her

to dress in that manner as an outward sign of her inner beliefs. But it took years before I learned that the Bible does not require women to wear black dresses with white collars in order to have a holy heart!

We must be careful not to view holiness through the eyes of our present culture. A dear friend said a coworker of hers approached her one day and inquired, "Mrs. L., aren't you going to wear these 'sinful' black stockings like the rest of us?" She displayed the latest designer hosiery for my friend to see.

"No," my friend replied. "You see, when I was a young girl, it was sinful *not* to wear black stockings!"

If we try to measure our holiness according to current world ethics, it will change daily, and we'll never know where we stand. We live in a world where we're expected to cheat on our income tax, find loopholes in the law, and take advantage of others. People cheat on husbands or wives, demand their rights, and claw their way to the top. Where does holiness fit in this realm?

You aren't the first one to wonder. The disciples also struggled with this question. Jesus reminded them:

> If the world hates you, keep in mind that it hated me first. If you belonged to the world, it would love you as its own. As it is, you do not belong to the world, but I have chosen you out of the world. That is why the world hates you *(John 15:18-19)*.

In fact, Jesus made this problem a matter of in-depth prayer when He prayed for His disciples (which also includes us):

> I have given them your word and the world has hated them, for they are not of the world any more than I am of the world. My prayer is not that you take them out of the world but that you protect them from the evil one. They are not of the world, even as I am not of it *(John 17:14-16)*.

The world we live in is not a holy place. It does not operate by holiness standards. When we stand for Christ, we will not fit into the world's mold. Yet Jesus expects us to be holy because He is holy, and He knows this holiness will separate us from the world.

Scripture also says:

> Do not be surprised, my brothers, if the world hates you *(1 John 3:13).*

Holiness will make us stand apart from the contemporary world around us. That shouldn't take us by surprise. We should expect it. How wonderful to know that 2,000 years ago Jesus prayed specifically about this problem. It gives me a strong sense of security to know that Jesus understands my problems and is praying for me.

It is clear that God commands us to live holy lives. He also expects us to move on to maturity in our spiritual lives.

> Therefore let us leave the elementary teachings about Christ and go on to maturity *(Heb. 6:1).*

The Book of Hebrews was written to encourage Christians to cultivate deeper spiritual lives. The author scolded the Christians for staying spiritual babies:

> We have much to say about this, but it is hard to explain because you are slow to learn. In fact, though by this time you ought to be teachers, you need someone to teach you the elementary truths of God's word all over again. You need milk, not solid food! Anyone who lives on milk, being still an infant, is not acquainted with the teaching about righteousness *(5:11-13).*

Being a vibrant Christian requires growth and maturity. It requires us to seek the deeper truths of Scripture and apply them to our lives. This growth process can only stop through our personal choice. As God presents new truth to us, we must choose whether or not to accept it. If we refuse it, we are turning our back on Christ.

My twin nieces were strapped into their matching high

chairs, hungrily eyeing the jars of baby food in their mother's hands. As each spoonful of food was offered to one, the other watched to see how her sister reacted. If one spit out the food, the other refused it too. This went on until hunger finally won out!

No matter how much food their mother offered, if they refused to eat, they would cease to grow. But even on milk alone the process wouldn't completely stop, leaving them babies forever. Instead, cells would begin to die, and eventually the lives that held such promise would be snuffed out.

To know that holiness exists and that God commands it, makes it a requirement. For new Christians, the knowledge of holiness may be lacking. But as God gives us knowledge, He begins working to fill our need of becoming holy.

It happened for the believers at Caesarea. First God sent an angel to speak to Cornelius, then He gave a vision to Peter, and finally He moved Peter from Joppa to Caesarea in order to meet the spiritual need of the people (see Acts 10).

It happened for the Christians at Ephesus. God sent Paul to speak to a dozen disciples who were unaware of the coming of the Holy Spirit.

> [Paul] asked them, "Did you receive the Holy Spirit when you believed?" They answered, "No, we have not even heard that there is a Holy Spirit" *(Acts 19:2).*

Paul explained to them the truths about Jesus and:

> When Paul placed his hands on them, the Holy Spirit came on them *(v. 6).*

To refuse growth, once God has given us knowledge, makes our refusal an act of disobedience toward God. We cannot remain neutral. We will either grow with the guidance of the Lord, or we will begin to deteriorate spiritually.

If we have to be holy, how holy do we have to be? Is it possible to pick and choose where and when each of us wants to be holy? As we learn new truths, there will be areas where we will not *exhibit* God's holiness until we bring those situations under His control through maturing. But in our relationship with God, there can be no partial holiness. It is either all or nothing.

As a Christian, can I say no if I don't want to live a holy life? Do I have a choice?

Scripture says:

> Do not be deceived: God cannot be mocked. A man reaps what he sows. The one who sows to please his sinful nature, from that nature will reap destruction; the one who sows to please the Spirit, from the Spirit will reap eternal life *(Gal. 6:7-8)*.

God knows whether we understand heart holiness. He also knows whether we have honestly accepted or rejected His offer of a pure relationship with himself. We may pretend to the people around us, we may even use all the right words and mimic the right actions, but it will only be a sham in His eyes.

If we reject God's offer, we will reap the consequences. But if we sow to please the Spirit, we will reap eternal life from the Spirit.

God always leaves the choice to us. He will not force us to accept His offer. We can say no if we want to. But we will reap destruction if we prefer self over pleasing the Holy Spirit.

The apostle Peter identified Christians in his First Epistle by mentioning the two steps of faith we've been discussing. He wrote to God's elect:

> Who have been chosen according to the foreknowledge of God the Father, through the sanctifying work of the Spirit, for obedience to Jesus Christ and sprinkling by his blood: Grace and peace be yours in abundance *(1:2)*.

If we are to be God's elect, we must have pure hearts, sanctified through the work of the Spirit. "Sanctified" means to be made holy, to separate to God or to a holy task. We are to be set apart for a special purpose. In this verse the purpose is identified as being *obedient to Jesus Christ.*

The apostle Paul declared the will of God to the Christians at Thessalonica when he said:

> May God himself, the God of peace, sanctify you through and through. May your whole spirit, soul and body be kept blameless at the coming of our Lord Jesus Christ. The one who calls you is faithful and he will do it *(1 Thess. 5:23-24).*

God calls us to be holy, and He is faithful to do exactly what He says He will do. He has the power to keep us pure and blameless until Christ comes again.

I sat near the front of my church, listening to a sermon on God's call to become holy people. At first it seemed like all the other sermons I'd heard on the subject, but then something began to happen inside me.

I was as committed to God as I knew how to be, having accepted Christ as my Savior when I was a child. But lately —in fact, for quite some time—I'd sensed that I was struggling harder and harder to please Him. Spiritually I felt exhausted with trying to do all the good I knew how to do.

As I listened to the sermon with one ear, God turned my other, inner ear to His voice. "You're struggling to do it all on your own. Let Me wear the other half of your yoke." His whisper grew louder, and my desire for the spiritual "rest" He offered grew more intense.

"You can't live the holy life through your own effort," He went on. "Let Me restore the purity of heart you need. Let Me *be* holiness within you. I am holy. When you let Me dwell in you, I become the purity you need."

In that moment I wanted nothing more than to be so totally committed to God that nothing else was of importance. My goals, my plans, my family—even my very life—held no value compared to the depth of commitment I wanted. In the haze of listening to two worlds I sensed an altar call was being given. I knelt and poured out my desire to Him.

"All that I am, all that I have, all that I ever will be, I now yield to You, Lord. I ask for Your Holy Spirit to indwell me." It was such a brief prayer I hardly realized it was over. Yet God saw my heart and knew I meant what I said.

I can't describe exactly what happened at that moment. It wasn't overpoweringly emotional, yet there was an exchange of emotion between God and me. There was a deep sense of assurance in my heart that God had fulfilled His promise. In truth and honesty I had asked for the Holy Spirit. In truth and honesty God had granted the request. It was now a fact! It was done!

When we say yes to God's call to holiness, we go through three steps. The first one is to acknowledge our deep need and ask God for the Holy Spirit.

> If you then, though you are evil, know how to give good gifts to your children, how much more will your Father in heaven give the Holy Spirit to those who ask him! *(Luke 11:13).*

The next phase is to wait before the Lord. There is a period of time, completely different for each individual, between our moment of asking and the fact of receiving. For some it is but an instant, for others it may involve a longer period of time.

It isn't that God is withholding His gift from us to be cruel or to cause us anguish. There may be some specific things we need to bring to Him for confession, restoration, or yielding of control into His hands.

Many times it's in the waiting that God works the best in us. Even for His disciples, Jesus indicated a waiting period. He could have had the Holy Spirit descend on them the moment He ascended into heaven, but He didn't. Instead, He declared a waiting time.

> I am going to send you what my Father has prom-
> ised; but stay in the city until you have been clothed
> with power from on high *(Luke 24:49).*

In other cases, as in the Christians at Caesarea, there
was an instantaneous outpouring of the Holy Spirit.

> While Peter was still speaking these words, the
> Holy Spirit came on all who heard the message *(Acts
> 10:44).*

When there is nothing left to lay before God in total
commitment, when we've yielded all there is to yield, the
last step is trust. Trust God to fulfill His promise. What He
says, He will do.

> But you will receive power when the Holy Spirit
> comes on you *(Acts 1:8).*

Notice the word "when." Jesus didn't say, *"If* the Holy
Spirit comes on you"; He said, "When." It is a fact. He promised the Holy Spirit, and He will give the Holy Spirit. The
promise is God's, the timing is God's, and the gift is God's.

This is a moment in our lives when we remove ourselves from the throne and yield the crown to the Holy
Spirit. It is willfully choosing to put the Holy Spirit in total
control of our hearts, dreams, desires, thoughts, and actions.

In that wonderful moment, we meet the Holy Spirit as
a Person. That meeting can be a surprise. I'm not exactly
sure what I expected, perhaps something like the iron rule
of a reigning monarch. Instead I was surprised by peace. Instead of the shackles of a slave, I found the joy of a Friend.

Before the collapse of the Soviet Union, with the assistance of a well-known Christian organization, a young
family left Russia, refugees because of religious persecution.
Less than 30 years old, the young husband and father had
already been imprisoned eight times for his faith.

He and his wife arrived in America with three small
boys, not knowing a single person. But God, who was their
Guide and Comforter, sent aid. A young Christian couple

met them at the airport along with other Christians. This couple took the Russian family into their home, fed and loved them, and ministered to their needs.

Within moments of meeting each other, the love of God flowed so openly between these couples that strangers became friends and eventually as close as brothers. One family came alongside the other family to comfort and give aid.

Before we yielded our lives to Him, the Holy Spirit was a stranger to us. But in that moment of commitment, the Stranger comes alongside to comfort us and give us aid, becoming a Friend who is closer than a brother.

In the length of a lifetime, we can't possibly discern all the personality traits of the Holy Spirit. His personhood within me is a constant source of surprise and discovery.

What we used to struggle so hard to do, now through His power becomes as easy as breathing. We don't have to try to live up to God's standards in our own strength. Now the power of the Holy Spirit shows us how to do it, making it possible to be the holy person God requires.

What makes this dramatic change? The Holy Spirit brings the greatest gift that was ever given, the love of God.

> And hope does not disappoint us, because God has poured out his love into our hearts by the Holy Spirit, whom he has given us *(Rom. 5:5)*.

Love is the evidence of holiness that we can expect in our lives. In fact, love is the only valid evidence of the Holy Spirit.

When the apostle Paul wrote to the Christians at Corinth, he showed them that nothing had any meaning without love.

> If I speak in the tongues of men and of angels, but have not love, I am only a resounding gong or a clanging cymbal. If I have the gift of prophecy and can fathom all mysteries and all knowledge, and if I have a

faith that can move mountains, but have not love, I am nothing. If I give all I possess to the poor and surrender my body to the flames, but have not love, I gain nothing *(1 Cor. 13:1-3)*.

Love is the universal gift of the Spirit. Everyone who is filled with God's Holy Spirit is also filled with God's love. It is this divine love in us that makes it possible to love the unlovely. It is this that allows us to love when love isn't returned. It even goes so deep as to cause us to love our enemies!

This kind of love is the pure love relationship with God that fulfills the greatest commandment: to love the Lord with all your heart, soul, and mind. It takes care of the next commandment, too: to love your neighbor as yourself (Matt. 22:36-39). The inner love brought by the Holy Spirit pours out through us and engulfs the universe.

The evidences of this love are known as the fruit of the Spirit. These will grow and become more clearly seen in our lives as the Holy Spirit lives in us.

But the fruit of the Spirit is love, joy, peace, patience, kindness, goodness, faithfulness, gentleness and self-control *(Gal. 5:22-23)*.

This kind of love doesn't seem to fit in today's society. But God's love through the power and person of the Holy Spirit makes it possible to live triumphantly in, and in spite of, our contemporary world!

* * *

THINK ON THESE THINGS

1. What specifically do you need to change in your everyday life (personal or business) in order to line up with Christ rather than the lesser standards of today's contemporary culture?

2. Discuss: "Do you have to be holy to be a Christian?"

3. Have you ever accepted God's offer of a pure relationship with himself through the Holy Spirit? If so, write the date of that experience here. _____.
(Note: some people can't recall the exact calendar date. In that case, put an estimated date on this line.)

Write a short description of that special moment:

4. In what ways has the Holy Spirit come alongside of you this week in order to comfort you or give you aid?

5. What specific thing is the Holy Spirit asking you to do this week in order to comfort or give aid to others?

6. How are you expressing God's love to those who might be considered your enemies?

7. What do you need to do in order to nurture the fruit of the Spirit in your life? Is there a specific one mentioned in Gal. 5:22-23 that needs special attention today?

*   *   *

Books to read:

Let Love Be Your Aim, Eugenia Price
The Mark of the Christian, Francis Schaeffer
These Earthen Vessels, W. T. Purkiser
Absolute Surrender, Andrew Murray

3

Commitment and the Excellent Choice

"I'm not sure I can tell you what happened to me." Anna struggled to describe her experience of yielding herself totally to Christ. "In one sense there was such utter peace in my heart, I knew I could trust God. But in another sense it was scary . . . and still is!

"I mean," she went on, "what if the Holy Spirit asks more of me than I can give?" She paused a moment, and her eyes dropped to her lap where her hands were tensely intertwined. "What if this is all just emotion?" Her voice softened. "What if nothing really happened and I just imagined it all?"

Anna isn't alone in her doubts. At some point in our lives all of us begin to question the reality of inner change. Some people have an emotional experience at the time of complete commitment, while others have absolutely none. But in either case, the authenticity of that moment with Christ can become suspect in our thinking.

So doubt is a natural emotion, and if we recognize it, we can learn how to deal with it. Think about it this way: Jesus cannot lie. Jesus himself promised the Father would send another Comforter, an inner witness to our faith.

And I will ask the Father, and he will give you another Counselor to be with you forever—the Spirit of truth. The world cannot accept him, because it neither sees him nor knows him. But you know him, for he lives with you and will be in you. I will not leave you as orphans; I will come to you. Before long, the world will not see me anymore, but you will see me. Because I live, you also will live. On that day you will realize that I am in my Father, and you are in me, and I am in you *(John 14:16-20)*.

Be assured that when you allowed Christ to ascend the throne of your life, that's exactly what He did. Name Satan for the liar he is, resist him (James 4:7), and choose to believe the truth of Christ's words.

But there is more to becoming holy women than this glorious moment of coronation. There is more than the overwhelming impact of meeting the person of Christ. The whole body is involved, not just the heart.

The apostle Paul says our bodies are to be living sacrifices. Fortunately he uses the word **living!** I think this means "living" more than just physical life; it means a lifetime of active, pulsating living. Sacrifice doesn't mean having an "I have given my life to Christ, so now I can just sit and do nothing" attitude. Nor does the sacrifice mean assuming a longfaced, "Woe is me! Look what I've given up for God" attitude.

Just as each person joyfully gives his or her body willingly and for a lifetime to one's mate in marriage, in the same way each person is to willingly offer his whole body to Christ.

It would be impossible to marry a person only in part. It takes the whole body, and that's true in this new spiritual relationship. Fingers, toes, tongue, eyes, and ears all now belong to the Lordship of Christ. Where we go, what we say, what we choose to view and hear, and even what we allow ourselves to think are now yielded to Christ.

We are no longer to live according to the pattern of this world. There is a new pattern, a new purpose, and a new plan for our lives. God's pattern, His purpose, His plan, are now ours. It is His gift to us; He ordained it before we were ever born.

> For you created my inmost being; you knit me together in my mother's womb. . . . All the days ordained for me were written in your book before one of them came to be *(Ps. 139:13, 16)*.

It's quite an adjustment to suddenly be no longer responsible for ruling our own life. What assurance to know that Someone far more capable is in control! We no longer have to push and shove and manipulate to reach "the top" according to the world's standards. We can trust Christ for what is best.

Most people want to make good choices in life. Some aspire to live an upgraded, better life. They weigh decisions and often attempt a higher quality of life in what they do and what they become.

Is it likewise in the Christian walk? Are there grades of Christianity? Is it possible for some people to be good Christians, others to be better Christians, and a few to be best Christians?

Christianity isn't a matter of grades. Rather it is the living out of a personal commitment to Christ. He will not force himself on us, even after we have yielded the throne to Him. We still have the right to choose what we think, say, and do. A king may sit on the throne, but the citizens may or may not align themselves with the wishes and guidance of the monarch.

After we become a citizen of God's kingdom, we decide what kind of citizen we will be. We can figure out what it takes to get by, following the rules and being a mediocre citizen. Or we can excel. We can become committed to the King and to the purpose of the Kingdom. We can pass by good, better, and best and be catapulted into the life of excellence.

God will not force us to live a life of spiritual excellence. It's a choice we must make. But because it involves our whole body and not just our heart, the life of excellence often is defined by our actions. One way is to discriminate between good and better when it comes to how we spend our time.

Two ladies who belong to the same country club were recently talking about how they spend their time. One lady said she spends her leisure time with her bridge club. She practices diligently and prepares carefully for each club meeting, grooming her house and herself meticulously.

The second lady mentioned that she has helped form a sewing club. Her sewing club ladies meet once each week to make clothes for poor children. Some bring their knitting, while others bring a portable sewing machine or handwork to finish. At Christmas the group supplied a complete outfit for each of nearly 400 children.

The contrast between the two seems extreme, but their stories are true. We can learn an important lesson from them. Both of those ladies had leisure time to spend. Both of them wanted to meet together with other ladies once a week, but one of them chose the more excellent way to spend her time.

As Christians, excellence needs to become our way of life. Not just in our leisure moments but in everything we think, say, and do. Stop and review your last 24 hours. Were there things you could have changed that would have caused you to live a more excellent life through the power of the Holy Spirit?

In the Book of 2 Corinthians, the apostle Paul challenges us to live more holy lives.

> Since we have these promises, dear friends, let us purify ourselves from everything that contaminates body and spirit, perfecting holiness out of reverence for God *(7:1)*.

We already have the promises. Now it's time to stretch

ourselves, to reach beyond what we are now and become holy women. Why? Scripture answers it best: "out of reverence for God."

Once Christ, through His Holy Spirit, is in charge of our lives, it's possible to live above the level of just getting by. The Holy Spirit *in us* is capable of pouring himself out through us so that each moment of our lives becomes vibrant with meaning. It's the Holy Spirit in us who will show us how to make the more excellent choices.

Leisure, of course, is only one part of our daily living. Excellence needs to permeate every aspect of our lives. Are there habits we need to change? Does our outward appearance reflect the excellence of Christ within us? Does our attitude of responsibility toward our homes, our jobs, our families, or other personal relationships display our devotion to God?

Commitment and the excellent choice begins in the careful disciplining of our spiritual life. Without a fresh, solid foundation, all our intentions are just ambitious goals.

Imagine waking up in the morning and bounding out of bed into the joy of a brand-new day. You throw open the curtains and declare to the brilliant sun, "Today I'm going to be excellent!"

Wrong! Purpose, goals, and determination are wonderful. We need them. But our plans should be carefully constructed on the bedrock of daily Bible reading and prayer. Trying to make excellent choices in a rough-and-tumble world without first talking with God is like walking out the front door without our clothes. Our worst flaws are fully exposed. Not only are we completely vulnerable to attack, but our condition actually invites it.

The first choice of excellence we make in the day is to open our Bible and read it. As we become available to God's input, He will reveal His guidance and His counsel.

Just as we can choose to begin our day with spiritual

food, we can also choose our mental diet. Have you ever been watering the garden, folding a mountain of laundry, or driving down the freeway, only to find yourself intently reviewing last night's television sitcom? The book you stayed up late to read or the soap opera that filled your afternoon impregnates your mental circuitry and bounces unbidden from subconscious to conscious level. In idle moments, mental or physical, our minds will work and rework the food we've given it.

Here, again, is another opportunity to allow the Holy Spirit to help us make the more excellent choice. Through His power we can choose excellence by filling our minds with the things of God. Does this mean we can never watch a sitcom or read a secular book? Of course not. But it does mean we are to submit to the controlling, guiding power of the Holy Spirit. How much better it would be to find our minds, in idle moments, dwelling on the nuances of Scripture or the majesty of God.

Excellence also includes disciplining our ears and mouth. We can develop selective hearing. If people are speaking words that do not reflect the love of Christ, we can react in three ways: (1) stay and listen, (2) excuse ourselves and walk away, or (3) stop the conversation and explain that we really don't want to hear what is being said.

As we allow the Holy Spirit to work in us, we'll learn how to react in each situation so that Christ will be glorified. It is through the love of Christ that we can turn our ears away from gossip. Through the power of the Holy Spirit we can choose not to listen to criticism of other people.

> The words of a gossip are like choice morsels; they
> go down to a man's inmost parts *(Prov. 18:8).*

You'd think we would choke on the delicacies some people offer on the silver platter of "I thought you'd like to know . . ." Instead, the Scripture says these gossipy words are delicious. We gobble them like the finest chocolates. We can justify hearing them just the same way we justify candy: "I really shouldn't have another, but since you were so thoughtful . . ."

Proverbs also reminds us,

> A gossip betrays a confidence; so avoid a man who talks too much *(20:19)*.

What we hear about people colors how we think about them. No matter how much we try to discredit negative statements or innuendos made about others, they still affect our thoughts. If we haven't *heard* the bad things, we won't have to work through them as we think about other people.

Let us be careful not to ignore the need for our own lips and tongues to be disciplined and cleansed. Isaiah was devastated when he measured himself against the purity of God's holiness.

> "Woe to me!" I cried. "I am ruined! For I am a man of unclean lips, and I live among a people of unclean lips, and my eyes have seen the King, the Lord Almighty" *(6:5)*.

The beginning of excellent choices in this area is to recognize that we need God's control and cleansing of our lips. The words we speak must constantly be sifted for truth and positive effect. We need to ask ourselves, "Do the words that pour from my lips truthfully portray other people and the character of God? Is there a carelessness of speech habits that dishonors Christ within me?"

Even our tone of voice needs to be submitted to the controlling power of the Spirit. The simple words "Yes, Dear" can slash your mate's life to shreds when wielded with an unholy tone. When a child has said, "Mommy, Mommy, Mommy," for the seven zillionth time, we can devastate him by screaming just one word, "WHAT?" in a tone that would curdle milk!

The Psalmist David knew that he needed to yield his

thoughts and his lips to the scrutiny of God's holiness when he said,

> May the words of my mouth and the meditation of
> my heart be pleasing in your sight, O Lord, my Rock and
> my Redeemer (19:14).

When a careless word or a harsh tone creeps into our speech, we need to take it quickly to Christ and ask Him to replace those words with ones that are pleasing in His sight. If we have a habit of using words or phrases that are not representative of Him, it may take some serious prayer and effort to change. But excellence in Christ is always an attainable and worthwhile goal.

Criticism seems to be one of the enemy's most effective and crushing tools. It slips off our tongues so quickly, destroys so completely, and can never be retracted no matter how hard we try. The old adage that says, "If you can't say anything nice about someone, don't say anything at all," is sound advice.

The more excellent choice is to graciously affirm people around us, believing the best about them, not tearing at them with a critical tongue. When tempted to criticize someone, we should instead pray for them. As we pray for them, we can ask God to extend His love to them. When done in sincerity, it's difficult to criticize that one we are praying for.

Having prayed for them, we can graciously affirm that person when an opportunity presents itself. Furthermore, every chance we get, we can talk to other people and tell them about the good points of this person. When we say good things about a person, it's amazing how quickly criticism dies unspoken on the listener's lips.

Be cautious with what you hear and speak! Holy ears and holy mouths are our best defense in a harsh world.

To complete the commitment of the whole body, we need to concentrate on the hands and feet as well. What we do and where we go are extremely important as we allow the Holy Spirit to guide us.

Hold your hands out in front of you and ask yourself, "If these were God's hands, what would they be doing?" Think about the types of things your hands do. Do the actions of your hands represent God's best?

Hands touch and hold, create and guide. Do our hands touch other people in anger and selfishness or in gentleness and love? What do our hands pick up and hold? Are those things that are clutched tightly the things that glorify God? Do the things our hands create bring honor or shame to the name of Christ? When our fingers point out a path to others, does that path lead them to Christ?

You may find it takes some constant attention from you to choose the more excellent actions for your hands. The hands of the Carpenter worked hard in an honest and respectable task to help support His earthly family. Those hands also caressed children and folded in prayer. They touched the eyes of the blind and beckoned people to salvation. Are we allowing Him to continue the same tasks through the use of our hands?

It's one thing to select "good" things to do. It's another to yield our choice to God and allow Him to make the selection. There was nothing wrong with the occupation of the disciples who were fishermen. But when they yielded to Christ, His choice of excellence for them was to become "fishers of men." What a difference their lives made after allowing Him to make the selection.

Sometimes it's not the task we do, but the *way we do it* that makes the difference. Zacchaeus, the tax man, worked for the local Internal Revenue Service. His job, although unpopular, was necessary to the work of the government. He did things the way everyone else did, looking out for himself and his personal gain. But when he met Christ, his whole attitude changed.

> Zacchaeus . . . was a chief tax collector and was
> wealthy. . . . But Zacchaeus stood up and said to the Lord,
> "Look, Lord! Here and now I give half of my possessions
> to the poor, and if I have cheated anybody out of any-
> thing, I will pay back four times the amount." Jesus said
> to him, "Today salvation has come to this house" *(Luke
> 19:2, 8-9).*

The attitude of Zacchaeus who had now yielded himself to Christ made the difference in *how* he handled his job.
From that time forward the tax collector's hands would
handle the tasks according to the more excellent choice.

How do you spend your time? Whether in work or in
play, are the things your hands find to do reflecting God's
choice of excellence? Have you taken time to *ask* Him what
He wants you to do? Are you being obedient to His choice,
or have you allowed yourself to settle for your own percep-
tion of doing good?

Christ's feet led Him to the Temple, to the home of
hurting people, to the wilderness, to the Cross. There was a
purpose and a plan behind everything He said and did, as
well as everywhere He went. From the hills of Galilee to the
bustling city of Jerusalem, Jesus deliberately orchestrated
His steps according to His Father's best plan.

Think about every place you've gone in the past 24
hours. Examine each choice carefully. Why did you go
there? Were your choices yielded to God's direction?

When we make the more excellent choice through deliberately submitting our bodies, wills, and actions to the
power of the Holy Spirit, our quality of life will change dra-
matically. We will gain purpose and direction. We'll leave
behind us mediocrity and uncertainty. We will be suddenly
free of the pressure to "do everything" and find ourselves
released to concentrate only on what God has chosen.

In spiritual matters, holiness *is* excellence. Why settle
for spiritual mediocrity? If you have already committed

your life to the direction of the Holy Spirit, are you willing to make the choices that will move you beyond best and into excellence?

Let us choose to become women who are disciplined in our spiritual lives through daily Bible reading and prayer, rather than allowing the chaos of emotional whims or lethargy to rule us. Does this mean we should isolate ourselves from the world? Of course not. We can choose to walk on a higher level than we've ever walked before. The Bible says,

> Seek ye first the kingdom of God, and his righteousness; and all these things shall be added unto you *(Matt. 6:33, KJV)*.

The woman of excellence can make the discriminating choice of taste between what is good and what is best.

*　*　*

Think on These Things

1. Are you just getting by as a Christian or have you committed your life to excellence through the Holy Spirit?

2. What specific things can you change in your present life pattern that will reflect the more excellent choice in how you spend your time?

3. Name the regular TV programs you watch or the type of books you read or both. How do these measure up to the mental food of excellence in the light of the Holy Spirit's guidance?

4. What speech habits do you need to change (bad language, gossip, criticism, etc.)?

5. (Personal) Name a person that you have recently criticized. Now begin immediately to honestly pray for that person, asking God to bless, guide, and shower this person with His love.

6. List what you do with your hands. Evaluate that activity in the light of God's excellence.

7. Is it necessary to ask God for guidance before you go anywhere or do anything? Why?

*   *   *

Books to read:

The Practice of the Presence of God, Brother Lawrence
In His Steps, Charles Sheldon
Living Above the Level of Mediocrity, Charles Swindoll

4

Walking in Holiness

"I want to make the right choices as a committed Christian." Jane spoke pensively, stirring her glass of lemonade. We sat on the patio of a local restaurant, letting the warmth of the autumn sun chase away the morning chill. "But sometimes I just don't know which choice to make. I can't tell the difference between two things that appear to be equally right."

The ice clinked in her glass as she thought deeply. "If Jesus were sitting right here at this table, I'd ask Him and expect to hear an answer. But He isn't here, so how can I know what to do?"

Jane's question isn't a new one. Whether you are a new Christian or one who has already yielded your life completely to the control of the Holy Spirit, you will always be searching for God's guidance.

Choices will always be with us; we can't escape making them. But *how* we make our choices, the reasoning behind them, involves a choice in itself. It is the choice to grow and mature in the holy life. Growth involves change and effort. Immature ideas, habits, and life-styles will be discarded for more mature ones. But God doesn't leave us to struggle alone through trial and error. He has provided a clear path.

A caterpillar doesn't suddenly become a butterfly. Instead, in the quiet, hidden resources of its cocoon, its Creator brings about the necessary changes. Butterflies don't grow in a day; neither do Christians mature in an instant.

We all need some cocoon time.

The metamorphosis may come slowly, but it will surely

happen if we take time to get alone with God. Hidden away from the eyes of the world, in the quiet presence of the Holy Spirit, we are changed.

In the cocoon, God prepares us for the days ahead. He teaches us the depth of His desires for our lives. As we pray and study His Word, He gives us the aids to help us grow spiritually.

Most of us pray, but we pray with such laxity and wanderings of mind that we leave our quiet place frustrated and feeling that we have failed to draw down blessings from heaven. Sometimes it seems our prayers become little more than wishful thinking. Jesus' disciples probably experienced many of the same misgivings. For them, prayer was little more than the form prayers they'd learned as children. But they saw a difference in Jesus. It was His habit to go alone and pray, sometimes all night. For Him, prayer was a way to converse with the Father, and He drew on it regularly. Eventually the disciples became curious about the transaction between Jesus and God the Father:

> One day Jesus was praying in a certain place. When
> he finished, one of his disciples said to him, "Lord, teach
> us to pray, just as John taught his disciples" *(Luke 11:1)*.

Some things are caught better than taught, and Jesus had waited until the disciples perceived a difference and wanted to learn. They had caught the idea that for Jesus prayer was different from what they were experiencing.

The prayer Jesus taught in answer to the disciples' request wasn't meant to be simply recited. He offered it as their model, something to use as a place to begin. In Matthew's version of what we call the Lord's Prayer, Jesus begins by saying,

> After this manner therefore pray ye *(6:9, KJV)*.

The problem with learning this prayer is that many people stop here. They learn it and recite it and that's it. Sunday after Sunday, service after service, out of habit, people parrot the words. But they really aren't praying.

Other scriptures give additional examples of how to pray. In the prayer of Jesus recorded in John 17, Jesus didn't simply recite the Lord's Prayer but prayed in depth for the disciples as well as each one of us.

To this model prayer as it appears in Luke's Gospel, Jesus adds another example. He gives the story of the man who needed to provide food for unexpected company in the middle of the night. This man went to his neighbor for help. He received the bread he needed, not because of their friendship, but rather because of his persistence.

Jesus adds the words,

> So I say to you: Ask and it will be given to you; seek and you will find; knock and the door will be opened to you. For everyone who asks receives; he who seeks finds; and to him who knocks, the door will be opened *(Luke 11:9-10).*

Jesus declares that it's not enough to ask. We are to continue asking until the request is granted. This doesn't mean badgering God. Nor does it mean He is deliberately taunting us by withholding His answer. But our fervent seeking of His will indicates we are getting serious with Him.

Early in the 18th century, there was a critical hour in the life of the Church. Martin Luther, John Calvin, and others had done their work in an earlier century, but now the Protestant believers were in confusion. Persecution was rampant. A man named Count von Zinzendorf decided to open the doors of his great estate in Herrnhut, Germany, to the persecuted evangelicals of Europe. At his invitation, Christians poured in from far and near.

Zinzendorf was a Christian who had a deep relationship with God. He had a burning desire to reach out to foreign countries with the message of Christ. The count spent entire nights pleading their cause in prayer. Others soon caught the spirit and joined him.

In 1727 they began praying around the clock, with large groups taking their turns, 24 hours a day for *10 years*. The results were overwhelming. In the next 25 years, 100 missionaries had gone to all corners of the earth.

John Wesley went to observe these people who were known as the Moravians and discover for himself what the Lord was doing. He sent a letter to his friends at home, saying: "I have found a church in which one breathes the very atmosphere of heaven."[1]

Zinzendorf didn't just ask—he persisted. He didn't badger God with rote prayers recited daily; he pursued the power of God with confidence and diligence. Others caught his vision.

Releasing the power of God in our lives involves fervent asking and persistent seeking. The Bible also tells us to *knock* that the door might be opened. Sometimes we need to knock on a lot of doors before we find the one that is God's answer to our prayers. Our strength in God's kingdom is directly proportional to how seriously we persist in knocking.

Martin Luther, when once asked what his plans for the following day were, answered: "Work, work, from early until late. In fact, I have so much to do that I shall spend the first three hours in prayer."[2]

The combination of serious prayer and active involvement in God's solutions is a winner. God expects us to be involved in the answers to our prayers. David Brainerd, the first American missionary to American Indians, often spent as much as four hours a day in prayer before he even began his daily work. Neither Martin Luther nor David Brainerd prayed and then sat back waiting for God to work. They believed in the combination that Jesus set forth in His life on earth.

> But the world must learn that I love the Father and that I do exactly what my Father has commanded me *(John 14:31)*.

Jesus prayed seriously and then worked hard, allowing God the Father to work through Him. He didn't just sit back and wait for people to come. He knocked on a lot of lives, looking for those who would open their heart's door to Him.

Are you "asking, seeking, knocking"? What would happen in your life, in your world, if you took those words seriously? Prayer is the single most important thing anyone on earth can do.

Let me talk just for a moment to my silver-haired sisters. You often say to me and to other leaders, "I just can't do much for God anymore. I'll have to let you younger ladies shoulder the load now."

Nonsense! You are the people who have the most experience in living, and you have the most knowledge. Don't you realize that it's significant that now, at this peak of experience and knowledge, God has given you the greatest task? He has removed from your shoulders the busywork that swallowed your time and energy for the past 60-plus years. In its place He has given you time and wisdom.

You, more than anyone else, know what needs to be covered in prayer. The only thing it takes is time and your choice. You don't have to be physically strong; you don't have to leave your home or spend hours in preparation. You can pray at any hour, in whatever your circumstances. All you have to do is close your eyes and focus on Jesus.

It sounds simple, and it is. But prayer is the greatest battlefield in the spiritual realm. It presents the greatest challenges and produces the greatest victories. The old-fashioned term *prayer warrior* means what it says.

When you pray, you enter into the thick of spiritual battle. In this case your silver hair becomes a great asset. Your years of life experience plus all your knowledge, combined with spiritual maturity and the guidance of the Holy Spirit, will win battles. Those who are younger and have less experience and knowledge will need your strength and power.

Don't use the excuse of age or infirmity to lay your burden down. Instead, pick up your shield and sword and wade into the heavy fighting! We need you!

The growing and maturing process also involves Bible study. Daily Bible study is not just a ritual. It is building a relationship with God. If we are going to worship God and allow Him to indwell us, we need to *know our God*. The Bible is where we learn about Him and learn *from* Him.

To *know* means to understand completely. It implies a relationship between the person knowing and the object known. We need this relationship between ourselves and God in order to understand Him and His love. Knowledge of this kind goes deeper than the intellect; it is obtained through the power of the Holy Spirit.

Bible study is extremely important in the holy life. Here, in the pages of God's Holy Word, we find His heart's desire for each of us. His guidance and direction for our lives are laid out clearly within its covers.

> Your word is a lamp to my feet and a light for my path *(Ps. 119:105)*.
> I will instruct you and teach you in the way you should go *(Ps. 32:8)*.

Jesus used the Scriptures to teach His listeners about himself.

> And beginning with Moses and all the Prophets, he explained to them what was said in all the Scriptures concerning himself *(Luke 24:27)*.

And, the Scriptures today are still useful for all manner of instruction:

> All Scripture is God-breathed and is useful for teaching, rebuking, correcting and training in righteousness *(2 Tim. 3:16)*.

It's from the Bible, during our quiet time, that God provides the soul nourishment that we need:

> Man does not live on bread alone but on every word that comes from the mouth of the Lord *(Deut. 8:3)*.

And by memorizing those precious words, we learn how to refrain from sinning against God:

> I have hidden your word in my heart that I might not sin against you *(Ps. 119:11)*.

Not only does it act against sin in our lives, but the Bible becomes the great offensive weapon we need in the spiritual battle:

> Take the helmet of salvation and the sword of the Spirit, which is the word of God *(Eph. 6:17)*.

> For the word of God is living and active. Sharper than any double-edged sword, it penetrates even to dividing soul and spirit, joints and marrow; it judges the thoughts and attitudes of the heart *(Heb. 4:12)*.

Through the power and direction of the Holy Spirit, we, the Bride of Christ, are made holy by God's Word:

> To make her holy, cleansing her by the washing with water through the word *(Eph. 5:26)*.

Often it seems deep and dark in our daily lives. Sometimes we feel so enclosed we can't see where we are going. In those times, it's God's Word that provides the light, the hope, that will keep us from stumbling.

> For everything that was written in the past was written to teach us, so that through endurance and the encouragement of the Scriptures we might have hope *(Rom. 15:4)*.

When I was a young girl, my mother gave me a pretty white Bible and penned a scripture inside the back cover. That verse has become my motto and goal.

> Study to shew thyself approved unto God, a workman that needeth not to be ashamed, rightly dividing the word of truth *(2 Tim. 2:15, KJV)*.

This verse is a command. It is not an option in the believer's life. We cannot live the holy life unless we know what God wants from us. In Scripture we find commands to obey, examples to follow, promises to claim, and warnings to heed.

Each of us needs to discover the best way to study the Bible in order to enhance our holy lives. Read carefully. Try to discover what the writer actually meant by using a Greek and Hebrew dictionary, footnotes, and cross-references. Study in several translations. Compare notes from several commentaries. Keep a daily prayer and Bible study diary, jotting down scriptures and thoughts.

Another important step is to discover what that passage of Scripture means today and how it applies to your personal life. Never lift a scripture out of the context of the *whole* Bible to make it say only what you want to hear! Beware of others who try to do exactly that! A good student of Scripture will listen to a speaker with a discerning ear, keeping in mind the whole context of the Bible.

Just as studying the Scripture will enable us to discern whether a message, written or spoken, is in full alignment with the whole of God's Word, so we need also to become discerning in other areas.

I listened recently to a radio message by a well-meaning minister as he spoke about material wealth. He had read a book that taught that all Christians should expect material prosperity. I wish that message were true. I know a lot of precious saints of God who could benefit greatly from that idea. But discernment, in light of the whole Word of God, shows it is a false teaching. If living a holy life produces material wealth, why was Jesus not wealthy? He who was holy, the Son of God, should have been the richest man in the world. But He wasn't. The message isn't true in the whole context of Scripture.

Walking in holiness involves becoming spiritually

aware. We will listen with "Spirit" ears; we will "see" through the eyes of the Holy Spirit. Although this ability is given to us through the Holy Spirit, awareness is also something we consciously cultivate. As we do, we'll begin to know the heart of God. It's like having an open telephone line to God's throne. We'll become more sensitive to the whispers of the Holy Spirit throughout the day. Little things, easily missed by the less sensitive, will take on spiritual significance as the Holy Spirit enhances our awareness.

A major gateway on the holiness pathway is labeled: Seeking God's goals.

When I first began writing professionally, my only goal was to be actually paid for my work. I wrote anything and everything I could think of, although I hasten to assure you that all of it reflected God's standards! I wrote articles about Western art and a weekly column on antiques. The more I wrote, the more ideas and possibilities for writing piled up. I have file drawers full of potential articles and books.

But the time came when God began speaking to me about my goals. Under the guidance of the Holy Spirit, I began to sense God wanted me to change them. Instead of writing to be paid, He presented the idea of writing to please Him. What a change! Suddenly every idea, every market, came under scrutiny. Was this article pleasing to God? Did it meet His goals? Did it enhance His kingdom, further the cause of the gospel?

> And whatever you do, whether in word or deed, do it all in the name of the Lord Jesus, giving thanks to God the Father through him *(Col. 3:17).*

This concept changed my life. Replacing my personal goals with God's goals created a whole new focus for me. As I worked on things other than writing, I continued to seek God's goals in these new areas too. What once was overpoweringly important faded to nonexistence and was replaced by new, Christ-centered objectives.

Two goals or choices may appear equally right. It is possible to discern the best by listening to the heart of Christ. We need to allow His view, His purpose, His goal to shape and mold our decisions.

In all of this, I have made a unique discovery. God's goals are much more interesting and exciting than mine. They are more challenging, more valuable, and far more lasting than anything I had ever concocted.

Walking in holiness also involves corporate worship, meeting together with other Christians for the purpose of worshiping God. This, again, isn't an option. The writer of the Book of Hebrews fits the idea of meeting together with other believers under the heading of encouragement.

> And let us consider how we may spur one another
> on toward love and good deeds. Let us not give up meet-
> ing together, as some are in the habit of doing, but let us
> encourage one another *(10:24-25)*.

Worshiping with others reminds us that we are not walking alone. It also helps us learn what other people are doing, how they are coping, and thus encourages us in our daily living.

Have you ever sat in a service and felt as if you just weren't worshiping God as adequately as you should? As you deal with this sense of inadequacy, recognize it might not be a lack on your part. Rather, it may be because you realize how much *more* He is and deserves, even when you've given all the worship ability that is within you.

One of the most valuable tools of worship is praise. Praising Him will help overcome this sense of inadequacy. I believe our greatest acts of worship come through praise. Just as God is infinite, so our praise and worship of Him can never be exhausted.

The more we praise Him, the more He reveals himself to us. The result is more reason to praise Him.

There is a power in praise that is released both in our hearts and into the universe that is unavailable by any other means. Praising God in adverse circumstances isn't easy, but it may be the one sure way of turning our personal world around.

Am I saying you have to praise God for the death of a loved one or because your teenager is on drugs? No, but I am saying that it's possible to praise God *in* and because of that situation. You can say, "God, I don't know *why* I'm in this situation, but I praise You for Your strength that is sustaining me." Later you will be able to praise Him for how He uses that situation when you allow Him access to every area of your life.

There were some dark days when I had no idea where my teenage daughter was or even if she was alive. During that time, my greatest strength and solace came from God. Now, years later, I can praise Him because those days taught me lessons I would not have learned any other way. I can reach out in true compassion to other parents who are hurting, people who need to know that God still cares. I could never have expressed this depth of compassion without my own experience.

There is a spiritual abundance that many Christians never reach because they do not choose to grow and mature. The challenge to each of us is to appropriate this abundance through a life committed to holiness. We are not to rest in our knowledge that Christ saved us from sin. We are to grow up in Christ (Eph. 4:11-16). We are to move on—become all we can be as a Christian!

> And beside this, giving all diligence, add to your faith virtue; and to virtue knowledge; and to knowledge temperance; and to temperance patience; and to patience godliness; and to godliness brotherly kindness; and to brotherly kindness charity *(2 Pet. 1:5-7, KJV).*

The Holy Spirit will aid us in this maturing process,

but the responsibility belongs to the individual to choose to "go on to maturity" (Heb. 6:1). Know that there is always *more*. We cannot exhaust God. The possibilities are endless to the person who makes a conscious effort toward improvement.

* * *

THINK ON THESE THINGS

1. Take a moment to identify the most pressing prayer need in your life. Write it in a prayer notebook. Are you willing to be part of God's solution to that prayer?

2. Name one person you can ask to pray with you about that prayer need. Contact this person this week to enlist prayer support.

3. To know exactly how to pray for another person, list the different items of prayer found in Eph. 3:14-19. (E.g.: 1. God will strengthen the person with power through the Holy Spirit [v. 16].)

4. How often do you regularly read the Scriptures? How can you change your current habit to provide more satisfying spiritual nourishment?

5. What goals that you have set for yourself need to be brought to God for His evaluation? As you pray about these, keep track of them in a prayer diary.

6. Name a circumstance where you can begin praising God either for His sustaining power or because He used it to teach you something new.

7. Are you bitter because of something in your past? Ask the Holy Spirit to show you how praise applies in that situation.

* * *

Books to read:

Purpose in Prayer, E. M. Bounds
Power Through Prayer, E. M. Bounds
Ordering Your Private World, Gordon MacDonald
Principles of Discipleship, Charles G. Finney

5

The Holy Mind

"I find myself thinking the strangest things at the weirdest times,"
Norene confided. "Like at church when the choir has just finished a
beautiful hymn and the pastor asks us to bow our heads in prayer
—and instantly I'm thinking about that new dress I saw down-
town! I should be praying and worshiping God; but instead I'm
wondering how to fit that dress into my budget, or whether I ad-
justed the oven temperature on today's dinner, or any of a dozen
other things."

The mind is a wonderful machine. It keeps working
even when we quit. Have you ever gone to bed at night only
to toss and turn for hours because your mind wouldn't quit?
Your mind can handle dozens of jobs at the same time. It
can be fully tuned to traffic as you drive down the road,
consciously working at controlling your car, and at the
same time keep track of what the kids are doing in the
backseat, handle a conversation with a friend, and suddenly
remind you to stop at the cleaners to pick up your husband's
suit.

But as wonderful as the mind is, it still needs someone
to be in charge, someone to set its priorities and channel its
energies. If you became too deeply involved in your friend's
conversation, you might miss the sound of your child trying
to open the car door. Or if you concentrated on what your
child is doing too fully, you might not remember to turn on
your signal light at the corner and end up in an accident.
Like the puppeteer with her dancing dolls or the computer

operator with her state-of-the-art computer, someone needs to be in charge and in full control.

My brother is a pilot for a major airline, and he tells me the newest, latest, greatest airplanes can do almost everything except wash the pilot's socks; but they still can't *think* for themselves! Someone has to tell the airplane what to do. What happens after that depends on the thought process of the pilot who made the choices. Will it fly or crash? Of all the reasons for plane crashes, "pilot error" is still the most frequent cause. No matter how magnificent the flying machine is, it still requires a pilot to be in control.

Exactly who controls your mind? Most of you would answer that question by saying, "I control my own mind." That's true in that you choose first of all whether you will submit your mind to the sinful nature, as we've discussed, or to the control of the Holy Spirit.

> Those who live according to the sinful nature have their minds set on what that nature desires; but those who live in accordance with the Spirit have their minds set on what the Spirit desires *(Rom. 8:5)*.

The first choice, then, is "Does sin or the Holy Spirit control my mind?" We determine first of all if we are a child of God, born into His family by the blood of Christ. Next, we ask, "Have I fully submitted myself to the indwelling presence of the Holy Spirit?" The answer to these two questions will tell us which control center is in command.

In the above verse, the apostle Paul was trying to explain to the new Roman Christians that their thought processes were the result of whatever controlled them. They would act and do whatever the command center told them to do. They did whatever pleased them.

Paul wanted them to know that a new Spirit was now in control of their lives. There was a new way to think, a new way to act, because the Spirit of Christ now indwelt them. He was teaching them to turn away from their former habits.

> And do not think about how to gratify the desires
> of the sinful nature *(Rom. 13:14)*.

He knew that the thought comes first and is followed by the act. So if they didn't think about how to gratify the desires of the sinful nature, then their actions would change. Paul contrasts the focus of the sinful nature with the mind that is controlled by the Holy Spirit. Rom. 8:5-8 lists the focus and problems of the "sinful mind": death, hostile to God, does not submit to God's law, can't submit to God's law, cannot please God. But he adds that those who live in accordance with the Spirit have their minds set on what the Spirit desires: not death, but life and peace (vv. 5-6).

The results of a sinful mind are shown in the Book of Ephesians. The apostle Paul says,

> So I tell you this, and insist on it in the Lord, that
> you must no longer live as the Gentiles do, in the futility
> of their thinking. They are darkened in their under-
> standing and separated from the life of God because of
> the ignorance that is in them due to the hardening of
> their hearts. Having lost all sensitivity, they have given
> themselves over to sensuality so as to indulge in every
> kind of impurity, with a continual lust for more *(4:17-
> 19)*.

Notice that the fall begins with futility of thinking. The decline proceeds through darkened understanding, separation from the life of God, ignorance, and hardening of their hearts. It ends in lost sensitivity, a life of sensuality, and indulgence in every kind of impurity, which never satisfies.

This decadent last state all began with an impure mind. The thought process determines our attitudes and our actions. If God does not control the mind, we are on a never-ending downward spiral.

Our relationship with God is also determined by our minds.

> Once you were alienated from God and were enemies in your minds because of your evil behavior *(Col. 1:21)*.

> But to those who are corrupted and do not believe, nothing is pure. In fact, both their minds and consciences are corrupted. They claim to know God, but by their actions they deny him. They are detestable, disobedient and unfit for doing anything good *(Titus 1:15-16)*.

The Lord contrasts the two minds in the Old Testament:

> The Lord detests the thoughts of the wicked, but those of the pure are pleasing to him *(Prov. 15:26)*.

We can allow our minds to be used by the sinful nature, or we can submit our minds to the Holy Spirit. We are personally responsible for the control of our minds. We can't blame our choice on anyone or anything else. Each one of us alone makes this decision.

Thoughts sometimes are so fleeting. They flicker through our minds and are gone. Often I find myself searching for an elusive thought. I'll think of some wonderful phrase or combination of words to use, but if I don't write them down immediately, they are gone. No matter how hard I try to recall them, they are lost forever!

Other thoughts seem to move in, set up camp, and stake a claim. At times when I need to be concentrating fully, my mind sticks on one subject and stays there. Today I'm trying to concentrate on submitting my mind to God. But I'm fighting thoughts of a vacation on a sun-drenched island in the middle of the Pacific Ocean!

Controlling our thought life is possible through discipline. In Scripture we are told to take charge of our minds.

> We take captive every thought to make it obedient
> to Christ *(2 Cor. 10:5)*.

My computer has a device embedded in its program that can pop up a message at set times, much like an alarm clock. I can be typing furiously, only to be interrupted by a mind-jarring beep and a flashing message. I have to stop what I'm doing and adjust myself to whatever that message reminds me to do.

We need to do the same kind of thing with our thoughts. If left unchecked, they will run out of control. But if we will, we can snare those thoughts, capturing them and bringing them under control. As thoughts of warm, sandy beaches pour through my brain, I must bring them into control and obedience to Christ.

Does that mean it's wrong to think about relaxing on a vacation? No, but as I capture those thoughts and make them obedient to Christ, I'll set them aside for a more proper time, such as when I'm ironing or washing dishes.

What if a bad or evil thought hits our minds? We do the same thing: capture it and bring it to Christ. We can be instantly in prayer and ask the Holy Spirit to remove this thought and replace it with His holiness. We do not have to allow the thought to stay and set up camp. Control is possible through the power of the Holy Spirit, but we must be actively involved.

In learning to discipline our minds with new thought patterns, we choose deliberately what we will think about. When an evil or bad thought enters, we replace it with thoughts of God. A good tool for accomplishing this is Scripture memorization. When our thoughts are running on idle, we can open the Bible and choose a new verse to memorize. This is a great aid in bringing our thoughts captive in obedience to Christ.

If our mind is overwhelmed with anxiety, we can bring it back into calmness by quoting Scripture. Choose promises in the Bible that apply to your situation, and allow the discipline of holy thinking to restore your mind.

When I was learning to fly an airplane, my instructor often said, "Practice doesn't make perfect; practice makes permanent!" What we do over and over again becomes a permanent pattern in our lives. If we repeatedly do something wrong, we will continue to do it wrong. If we repeatedly train ourselves to control our thoughts, we will find them becoming more and more under the control of the Holy Spirit.

As we develop a new pattern of thinking, we guard carefully what we put into our minds. What we see and hear becomes indelibly etched on our memory. We'll rerun what we've seen and heard, without consciously making the choice.

My husband was driving across town recently humming a very catchy tune, when it suddenly caught my attention. "Do you know what song you're humming?" I asked.

"No, just something I heard on the radio, I suppose," he answered.

When I told him what the song was and quoted some of the words, he was shocked. "I didn't even think about the words." He shook his head in disbelief. The song contained phrases of adultery, intoxication, and an anti-Christian view of heaven. Letting the radio play randomly or leaving the TV turned on may fill the air, but it may also fill your mind with strong anti-Christian thoughts.

A good example of Satan's subtle traps for our thought life is the daytime soap opera. If we spend our day engrossed in television romances, our minds will be filled with cheating, lying, adultery, divorce, extramarital relationships, hate, anger, and even murder. I guarantee we'll be angry at our husbands at least once a week if we watch soaps. We'll begin thinking they aren't attentive enough, or sexy enough, or rich enough to cater to our whims. We'll suspect they're having an affair if they are late getting home. The list is endless and leads only to destruction of our homes, marriages, and families.

The same holds true with reading "steamy" sex novels. I love to read good fiction, and I enjoy romantic novels. But I choose carefully what I read. Remember—garbage in, garbage out!

There's one more pitfall I'll mention. A number of Christians, in the secret of their closet, view pornographic material. They excuse it by saying, "It doesn't hurt anybody, and nobody needs to know." That is a lie.

Pornography destroys! To begin with, it hurts *you*. It fills your mind, hinders your relationship with Christ, and erodes your home. Pornography cannot be kept in the closet. Eventually it will spill out.

It is proven that pornography has played a major role in the lives of criminals. Just before his execution, admitted serial murderer Ted Bundy told Dr. James Dobson of Focus on the Family that he was addicted to pornography. A recent leader in Romania, who committed heinous crimes against thousands of people, was addicted to pornography.

And a pastor I know who left his wife, family, and congregation was also addicted to pornography.

It can happen to Christians.

You are what you think. The hurting doesn't stop with you; it extends to your family, friends, and acquaintances.

If you are a Christian who is caught in this terrible web, submit willingly to the Lord in a spirit of confession. Ask for forgiveness and healing. Seek professional help from a Christian counselor. God is waiting with open arms, but the choice is yours.

Each one of us needs to allow Christ to resurrect His life within our minds. God already knows our thoughts (Ps.

94:11). He is willing to renew every nook and cranny of our minds. The apostle Paul reminds us:

> But we have the mind of Christ *(1 Cor. 2:16)*.

When we yield ourselves to the control of the Holy Spirit, our minds become a throne for God's laws (Heb. 8:10). We know what God wants from us because His thoughts become our thoughts. King David reflected on the thoughts of God and marveled at them.

> How precious to me are your thoughts, O God! *(Ps. 139:17)*.

If God puts His thoughts into our minds, then what do we put into the mind that is yielded to Christ? The first thing to do is select our focus. We are reminded to:

> Set your minds on things above, not on earthly things *(Col. 3:2)*.

Then, we must choose the types of things to think about. The Bible tells us:

> Whatever is true, whatever is noble, whatever is right, whatever is pure, whatever is lovely, whatever is admirable—if anything is excellent or praiseworthy— think about such things *(Phil. 4:8)*.

We make deliberate choices about our thoughts. This can be especially helpful as we deal with the people whose lives intersect ours. As you consider friends in your neighborhood, acquaintances at church, and members of your family, do a little divine eavesdropping. When you see these people, put your own negative thoughts on "hold," and listen to what God is thinking about them. As God views them, His heart is overwhelmed. He loves each one so much He sent His Son to die for them. Think about them the way God does, and you'll change your whole point of view!

Negative thinking can drag you down and make your life joyless. But shifting your focus to the good in people and circumstances will generate a genuine optimism in your outlook.

Does this mean we must be mindless Pollyannas? By no means. I'm not suggesting a superficial switch or that we should ignore difficult circumstances. To be honest in our appraisals and still think positively, we must look beyond adversity and reach for God's thoughts on the subject. As we ask ourselves, "How does God view this person or situation?" the Holy Spirit can bring God's thoughts into our minds. The change is amazing. We'll discover insights into people and situations we never knew were there.

What else do we put into our minds? King David selected things that God had done in the past, those glorious divine acts of creation, guidance, leadership, and intervention. His thoughts focused on things about God that he had read in Scripture or had been taught in religious instruction. He thought about times when God had been active in his own life.

> I remember the days of long ago; I meditate on all your works and consider what your hands have done (Ps. 143:5).

When you have quiet moments, follow David's example and think about God. Recall times when God has intervened in your life, or meditate on Scripture.

As we renew our minds, we are transformed. Our new thought patterns will enable us to understand God's will. In fact, this change is a command in Scripture. Commands were given to be obeyed. We are told to:

> Be transformed by the renewing of your mind. Then you will be able to test and approve what God's will is—his good, pleasing and perfect will (Rom. 12:2).

As we yield our thoughts to the purifying and refining power of the Holy Spirit, God's peace will become a hedge, guarding our minds.

> And the peace of God, which transcends all understanding, will guard your hearts and your minds in Christ Jesus *(Phil. 4:7).*

There are some exciting results from this new way of thinking. The more we dwell on God, the less time we'll spend on negative thoughts. We won't worry and be anxious. God's peace will replace both of those patterns.

Another result is holy conversation. If we are "thinking God," we'll "talk God." What we think naturally flows into our speech. If we are focusing on things that are lovely and pure, our conversation will be above reproach. We can pray with the Psalmist:

> May the words of my mouth and the meditation of my heart be pleasing in your sight, O Lord, my Rock and my Redeemer *(19:14).*

Not only will our thinking and speaking change, but so will our actions. The apostle Peter admonishes us:

> Therefore, prepare your minds for action; be self-controlled; set your hope fully on the grace to be given you when Jesus Christ is revealed *(1 Pet. 1:13).*

Our life choices come because of the way we think. In the process of becoming holy women, each of us needs to answer clearly the question, "Who is in control of my mind?"

* * *

THINK ON THESE THINGS

1. List (for your eyes only) several normal things you do that support and define who is in control of your mind.

2. In order to bring your thoughts and mind into line with God, what changes do you need to make in your reading, listening, or TV viewing habits?

3. Select a passage of Scripture to memorize. Test yourself in a week. Write one new thought you've had because of thinking about this Bible verse.

4. What thoughts do you need to make obedient to Christ?

5. Make a list of things to think about that fit with the suggestions in Phil. 4:8.

6. Name some thoughts that lead to actions (e.g., anger leads to violence; thinking about God leads to prayer; etc.). How can these thoughts be brought under the control of the Holy Spirit?

7. List seven actions or attributes of God that are praiseworthy. Select one of these each day this week and deliberately choose to think about it. Keep notes that record your thoughts on each one, and review them at the end of the week.

*   *   *

Books to read:

My Utmost for His Highest, Oswald Chambers
The Reality of Prayer, E. M. Bounds
The Necessity of Prayer, E. M. Bounds
The Spirit of Christ, Andrew Murray
The Knowledge of the Holy, A. W. Tozer

6

Holy Attitudes

"They won't even allow your name to be included in the nomina-
tions?" Nancy was shocked.

"Because I'm a woman," Juanita affirmed. "I can be director of
the children's classes, but not for the whole Sunday School. The
church board wants a man in that position."

"What a bunch of stuffed shirts!" Nancy clenched her fists.
"Don't they know that kind of attitude went out with the Dark
Ages? If they tried that kind of action in the workplace, they'd get
sued. I wouldn't put up with their decision for even one minute!"

"It doesn't seem fair," Juanita agreed, "but as a Christian I
don't think I can fight it. In the secular world there is a clear line
on equal rights, but in the church . . ." Her voice trailed off, and she
let the sentence hang unfinished.

What is a Christian woman to do when she runs into a
women's rights problem in the church? It's easy to assume a
militant attitude, especially when women's rights issues are
so prevalent in the media today. The problem comes when
the secular and sacred worlds clash head-on.

"Women are to be quiet and keep their place," a man
recently told me. "That's what the Bible says, and that's the
final word!" He was referring to these verses:

> As in all the congregations of the saints, women
> should remain silent in the churches. They are not al-
> lowed to speak, but must be in submission, as the Law
> says *(1 Cor. 14:33-34).*

In looking up the word "speak" (Greek, laleō), I discovered a meaning that is overlooked or lost in our language today. Yes, it means "to talk, utter words," but it also carries a further meaning, including "an extended or random harangue."

The Bible, through the words of the apostle Paul, is saying women are not to dominate the church service in extensive talk or with an accosting attitude. That makes sense, and Paul is a common-sense person. If he had been talking about opening our mouths to "break silence," he would have used a different Greek word, which means to "utter, speak, or say."

Again, the Greek word for "keep silence" (KJV) means to "hold your peace." Church isn't the proper place to air grievances that could lead to division.

Attitude is the whole point of this passage of Scripture. What should our attitude be when we are confronted with a situation in church that seems unjust? Do we react with foot-stomping, bone-picking contention? Or is there a better way?

In the last chapter we talked about having the "mind of Christ" within us. Our attitudes need to reflect the thinking of Christ. How would He react to our particular situation?

When it comes to demanding a person's rights, Jesus is our primary example of how to react. Think about His situation for a moment. He, who was King of Kings and Lord of Lords,

> made himself nothing, taking the very nature of a servant, being made in human likeness *(Phil. 2:7)*.

Think of the rights He could have demanded when He came to earth. He was our Creator, yet He chose to be made "a little lower than the angels" (Heb. 2:9). He yielded His rights in order to provide a better way for us.

> For you know the grace of our Lord Jesus Christ, that though he was rich, yet for your sakes he became

poor, so that you through his poverty might become rich
(2 Cor. 8:9).

Jesus looked beyond the immediate. He knew He had
to yield His rights in order to provide eternal riches for us.
His attitude became one of selflessness and humility. He
gave no thought to demanding His rights.

Our greater need in the Body of Christ is to glorify God.
There will be times when we must yield our personal rights
in order to accomplish the greater task. There are times
when we can speak up and calmly, logically, present our
case. But we must always look beyond the immediate and
keep our focus on the final goal of glorifying God. It isn't
always easy to make this choice, but the results are worth it.

In the Old Testament, Abraham came to a point when
he knew it was best to yield his rights. He wanted to end
the disputes between his servants and the servants of his
nephew, Lot. As the elder, Abraham had the right to choose
first. But in an act of gracious yielding of his rights, he allowed Lot to make the choice.

> Is not the whole land before you? Let's part com-
> pany. If you go to the left, I'll go to the right; if you go to
> the right, I'll go to the left *(Gen. 13:9).*

It takes a strong person to yield her rights. This
strength comes from a solid relationship with God through
the Holy Spirit. If we are growing through daily contact
with Him, we will be able to determine the mind of Christ
in each instance. Being in close touch with God enables us
to know when to stand firm and when to yield.

Even when we make a conscious choice to yield our
rights, there is a fine line on *how* we yield them. It's easy to
yield with a miffed or whining attitude. Another undesir-
able method is the "chip on the shoulder" attitude, which
says, "I'm giving in this time, but just you wait until *next*
time!" Not once do we observe this kind of attitude in the
life of Christ. We should model our responses after the gra-

cious, loving yieldedness that characterized His life. Jesus says that the mark of the Christian is love:

> All men will know that you are my disciples if you love one another *(John 13:35)*.

The apostle Paul defines many of the facets of love for us in his first letter to the church at Corinth.

> Love is patient, love is kind. It does not envy, it does not boast, it is not proud. It is not rude, it is not self-seeking, it is not easily angered, it keeps no record of wrongs. Love does not delight in evil but rejoices with the truth. It always protects, always trusts, always hopes, always perseveres *(13:4-7)*.

I don't see anything in this list that says we can demand our own rights. In fact, it points rather clearly to the opposite action.

True holiness is love: first, love of God; and second, love for others. Have you ever seen a ray of sunshine strike a crystal prism? The resulting spectrum of glorious, rainbow color spreads over a wide area in beautiful diversity. That's the same principle of holiness. My love for God flows *through Him* and multiplies, spreading out to others.

If we nurture an attitude of love in our hearts, the results show in our lives. We also reap a harvest of peace rather than anger.

> A happy heart makes the face cheerful *(Prov. 15:13)*.

> But the fruit of the Spirit is love, joy, peace, patience, kindness, goodness, faithfulness, gentleness and self-control *(Gal. 5:22-23)*.

We have been talking about walking in love and humility. These are not to be confused with timidity or faint-heartedness. Instead, we are to be strong and bold as we allow the Holy Spirit to work through us.

How does this attitude of yielding our rights fit with the well-publicized women's movement of today? Are we to cower timidly in the face and force of NOW? Of course not!

Let's show the world what real women, women of God, holy women, can do.

Political action, social justice, etc., are not the *goals* of the holy but are an expression of the holiness within us. We need to boldly confront issues that are contrary to God's holiness, but in our boldness we need to be sure our attitude is that of Christ's love.

Love doesn't bomb an abortion clinic. But love will reach out to a pregnant woman and hold her hand, offering her the strength and caring she needs in her situation. God's love is compassionate, understanding, and healing.

There is a difference between yielding our rights and buckling under a browbeating pressure to submit. But if yielding isn't submission, then where does submission fit in the holy life?

This word *submission* is one most of us, even as seekers after godliness, do not like. The whole idea is generally repugnant. But when we analyze the truth, submission is a basic foundation to God's processes in our lives. First and foremost, we are to submit to God.

> Submit yourselves, then, to God. Resist the devil,
> and he will flee from you *(James 4:7).*

It is in our submission to God that we gain the power to resist the devil. Where would we be if we were unable to resist Satan? It's a frightening thought!

Next, we are to submit to those in authority:

> Submit yourselves for the Lord's sake to every authority instituted among men: whether to the king, as the supreme authority, or to governors, who are sent by him to punish those who do wrong and to commend those who do right *(1 Pet. 2:13-14).*

Another area of submission is to each other as members of the Body of Christ:

> Submit to one another out of reverence for Christ
> *(Eph. 5:21).*

One of the most-publicized areas of submission is in the marriage union:

> Wives, submit to your husbands as to the Lord *(Eph. 5:22)*.

Not one of these situations allows for browbeating by the party in control. Nor does it call for the one who submits to act as a doormat. Our submission to one another and to our husbands is one of an equal person willing to yield personal rights in order to glorify God and complete His tasks. Submission then becomes a question of our purpose. Are we set on accomplishing our own desires, or are we willing to follow God's plan?

Many of us will try to rationalize our lack of submission by saying, "But I'm doing God's work, and in order to accomplish this task, I can't submit!" We try to cover up the fact that we are accomplishing our own desires *first*.

Ideally, Christians would each submit to one another in equality and holy love, and both would be submitted to God. In that way, God's will is the ultimate goal of each one, and the submitting will be a delight. However, reality often paints a different picture. Not everyone is willing to submit, first to God and then in equal love to one another. That's where the problem is.

When those who are in authority are not in submission to God, they often take advantage of their subordinates. When those who should submit are seeking their own desires, their demands grate against the natural working of the Body of Christ. Neither of these attitudes reflects the attitude and example of Christ.

Yielding our personal rights, sincere self-denial, is an attitude of holiness. When we choose to deny ourselves something in order to place ourselves in the mainstream of God's holy will, we are displaying a holy attitude. Self-denial for self-denial's sake accomplishes nothing.

Attitudes make all the difference in the world in accomplishing any task. When we are willing to be a servant, not a star, we are allowing the Holy Spirit to work through us.

> Clothe yourselves with humility toward one another, because, "God opposes the proud but gives grace to the humble." Humble yourselves, therefore, under God's mighty hand, that he may lift you up in due time *(1 Pet. 5:5-6).*

> Humble yourselves before the Lord, and he will lift you up *(James 4:10).*

When we demand our own rights, we exalt ourselves. But, when we yield and submit in honest humility, the Lord will lift us up. What a difference!

It is possible to lose self-esteem when we are forced into submission by others or through inappropriate guilt. This is a problem that can arise when submitting is not handled in love and equality. It is easy to damage one another if we are not sensitive to the leading of the Holy Spirit.

Our personal worth is never devalued by God. He prizes us so highly that He sent His Son to redeem us, even when it cost Christ His life! If God values us that highly, we must treasure our personal worth. This is not exalting ourselves or being self-centered. Rather, it is viewing every person, including ourselves, through the eyes of God.

We need to do everything we can to help one another maintain a healthy personal worth. How we view ourselves affects how we view others and, ultimately, how we view God. If we are to live the holy life, we need to see ourselves and others as God sees us—very precious!

As precious as people are in God's sight, there are times when we act less than precious to one another. The Bible says:

> Be kind and compassionate to one another, forgiving each other, just as in Christ God forgave you *(Eph. 4:32).*

Hurts happen. Sometimes we can be hurt so quickly we hardly know how it occurred. Other times the hurt begins very small and slowly builds. In either case, our attitude is going to play a major role in the outcome. We can easily become angry and bitter when we've been hurt by other people.

Not only will our reaction and emotions focus on those who hurt us, but they will sometimes include God. "Why did You let this happen to me, God?" "How could You allow me to be hurt like this?" If we allow this thinking to continue, it will strangle our relationship with God.

When we have been hurt, the natural instinct is to lash out and hurt in return. But the woman who has committed her life to Christ will allow the Holy Spirit to react in her place.

We begin the process of recovering from our own hurt by choosing to trust God, no matter what has happened. Trust never demands an answer or explanation. We need to learn to say, "It's OK, God; if You never explain this to me, I'll still love You and trust You." When this attitude dominates our emotions, we allow God the freedom to work His best within us.

Then we turn our attention to the one who has caused the hurt. Whatever that person has done, we are to forgive. Those are tough words, especially when the hurt in our lives has been deep and long-standing. But if we don't forgive, it causes damage in our spiritual lives.

> And when you stand praying, if you hold anything against anyone, forgive him, so that your Father in heaven may forgive you your sins *(Mark 11:25)*.

From the smallest slight to the most horrendous crime against us, the command to forgive is the same. We choose what we will to do with this situation. Quite often our reaction will be to hold a grudge. Forgiveness doesn't always "happen."

We cannot cause the other person involved in the hurt to change her actions or attitude, but we can change our own reaction and attitude through forgiveness.

When forgiveness seems impossible—PRAY! Pray for your own attitude, and pray positively *for* the other person. How or what do you pray for a person who has caused you hurt? Begin by asking God to bless that person. Pray for good things to come into her life. Pray positively for her job, home, and family, as well as her spiritual life.

In the Sermon on the Mount, Jesus tells us what to do about people who persecute us:

> But I tell you: Love your enemies and pray for those who persecute you, that you may be sons of your Father in heaven *(Matt. 5:44-45)*.

In Luke's Gospel, He tells us we are not to retaliate when we have been mistreated:

> If someone strikes you on one cheek, turn to him the other also *(6:29)*.

God wants us to allow Him to bring healing into our lives in the middle of hurting relationships.

I stood on the platform of our church, giving a talk on the Ten Commandments. As an object lesson, I smashed each of 10 glasses with a hammer to emphasize that our lives are shattered when we violate God's laws. At the end of the talk, to demonstrate how God puts our lives back together when we seek His forgiveness, I lifted a whole glass from beneath the table and put it in place of each broken one. "God takes the broken pieces of our lives and makes us whole again," I said, ending the talk.

Later, I heard that an emotionally disturbed girl who had been sexually abused was sitting in the audience. It was her first outing from the hospital, and a counselor had brought her to church. The demonstration I gave that day was the springboard for some serious discussion between them about allowing God to heal the hurts in her life.

When I heard her story, I sent her one of the glasses I'd used so that she could have a visual aid in her healing process.

The young girl later attended an Esteem Conference, where she shared her story. Holding up the glass, she said, "I don't have to live my life in broken pieces. I can let God put the pieces back together."

She could not change her circumstances, but this devastated young girl made a conscious choice to allow God to heal her hurts. Attitude makes all the difference in the world! Although it may be difficult to bless those who mistreat us, for our own spiritual well-being we need to give our blessing anyway. There are others, too, who may not have mistreated us but have disappointed us. These people also need our blessing.

As mothers, do we ever unwittingly communicate an attitude of "I'll wait until you prove you're worth it before I'll give you my blessing"? This same attitude can prevail between other family members, church members, and co-workers in the workplace. We need to allow the Holy Spirit to flow through us and bless those who are a part of our lives. They need to know that, although we may not approve of their actions, they are loved, accepted, and forgiven —precious people in God's eyes.

Seeking to have a holy attitude, created by the Holy Spirit within us, is really part of the spiritual battle. Whether it covers "rights," "submission," "forgiveness," or any other attitude, the battle is real. This is spiritual warfare; so what is our best weapon? Prayer.

We have two choices—we can fight our enemies, or we can pray for them and bless them. This is the place where militance fits in our holy war. It takes strength to choose to pray for an enemy. Seasoned spiritual warriors have learned the value of a holy attitude. They know that yielding our rights, submitting, and forgiving are elements that forge the steel of our armor.

In the spiritual war involving our attitudes, there is a clarion call to Christian soldiers: "Join the Army!"

Where does the battle begin?

In your prayer closet—on your knees.

* * *

THINK ON THESE THINGS

1. What personal rights is God asking you to yield in order to meet the greater goal of glorifying Him?

2. What attitude is God asking you to yield to the power of the Holy Spirit? What do you think might happen if you allow Him to change your attitude?

3. What situation is God bringing to your mind where you are set on accomplishing your own desires? How can self-denial or submission change that situation so that you will be willing to follow His plan?

4. What can you do this week to enhance the self-esteem of someone close to you?

5. Is there an attitude of bitterness or anger in your life that you need to bring to God?

6. What situation or relationship in your life needs the healing of forgiveness? What situation or relationship needs the change of an attitude of blessing?

7. How do you plan to respond today to the call to join in spiritual warfare?

* * *

Books to read:

Hide or Seek: How to Build Self-esteem in Your Child, Dr. James Dobson
Love, Acceptance, and Forgiveness, Jerry Cook
Living Beyond the Daily Grind, Charles Swindoll
The Habit of Happiness, Leslie Parrott
The Power of Your Attitudes, Leslie Parrott

7

Overcoming Temptation

"Does a Spirit-filled Christian experience temptation?" Velma was honestly seeking an answer. "I thought the power of the Holy Spirit would prevent that problem. Either I'm not where I should be spiritually, or I'm going through some severe testing by Satan!"

Every day we are confronted in some way with temptation. Some of it is easy to resist, and some of it is tough to withstand. And some of it is so disguised that we don't recognize it until it is too late.

I'm glad Jesus went through the temptations in the desert and chose to include His experience in the Scripture for our example. Since He was alone in the desert, we can assume it was His choice to tell what happened.

It is interesting to understand the timing of Jesus' temptation. In a blaze of glory, Jesus had just been publicly verified by the voice of God Almighty after He had been baptized by John. Then He spent 40 of the most intensive days of His life alone with God in the wilderness. Wouldn't you think at that point in His life, He would have been so close to God that He wouldn't have heard temptation's slightest whisper? But though He was God, Jesus was also truly human.

Have you ever been working hard in a certain ministry or just enjoyed a mountaintop experience, only to be slammed into a confrontation that caused you to question the whole focus of your life?

By being aware of when temptations are likely to come,

we can be more alert and not caught off guard so easily. Have you just started a new ministry? Have you just had a mountaintop experience or a wonderful time of blessing? Be alert. You are a prime target.

> Then Jesus was led by the Spirit into the desert to be tempted by the devil. After fasting forty days and forty nights, he was hungry *(Matt. 4:1-2)*.

There seem to be three easily identified areas to watch for temptation to strike: pleasure, pride, and power.

Jesus was hungry. His body was in need of being satisfied. This first temptation involved the pleasure of taste. Although I've never gone 40 days without food, there are other, more subtle ways I've been tempted by the pleasure of taste.

I'm an admitted, card-carrying chocoholic. My family and friends are always sending me little cartoons about chocolate. If we pass a candy store, I need someone to hold my hands and firmly guide me on down the street. Of course, it doesn't have to be chocolate—anything with calories will do.

The holidays are perhaps the most difficult for me because everyone is baking, and there are more parties to attend than hours in a day. Food definitely provides a temptation to indulge in the pleasure of taste.

Another area of temptation is the pleasure of touch. "If it feels good, do it" is a rather coarse bumper sticker we often see. Personally, I'd rather touch silk and satin than burlap. But the subtle temptation is to indulge myself in the finer things when my budget won't quite allow it.

> Rather, clothe yourselves with the Lord Jesus Christ, and do not think about how to gratify the desires of the sinful nature *(Rom. 13:14)*.

The temptation of pleasure is revealed not only through taste and touch but also through our emotions. There is nothing wrong with taste or touch or emotions. We need all of these, but they fall under the heading of temptation when we are carried away by our own desires.

> But each one is tempted when, by his own evil desire, he is dragged away and enticed. Then, after desire has conceived, it gives birth to sin; and sin, when it is full-grown, gives birth to death *(James 1:14-15)*.

Temptation in itself is not sin. It is when we yield to temptation, when we give in to our desires, that sin enters our lives.

One emotion that could tempt us is romance. If we spend time fantasizing romantic thoughts, we'll begin to focus those thoughts on a specific person. James says we'll be "dragged away and enticed" by our own evil desire. When that romantic desire conceives, it gives birth to sin, and we'll take steps to make our fantasies reality. From there, unless stopped, the natural course of events will lead us to sin.

Another example could be the emotion of anger. If we allow anger to fill our thoughts, we'll focus that anger on a person. We'll be dragged away and enticed by that anger until it consumes us, and we'll take steps to gratify that anger. When we yield to anger, it will lead to sin, and the result of sin is death. Emotion of itself isn't bad, but when we let go of our control and yield to it, allowing it to entice us, we are on a downhill slide to sin.

It wasn't wrong for Jesus to want to eat. He needed sustenance, but under those circumstances it would have been wrong to yield the control of that emotion to gratify His human pleasure.

There's nothing wrong with wearing nice clothes if they fit into our budgets. And I'm glad God gave us the emotion of romance, but it belongs in the controlled situation of a marriage.

All of us have been tempted in these areas at some point in our lives. For you, chocolate may hold absolutely no temptation, but it may be some other type of food. Perhaps indulging in the pleasure of touch doesn't involve silks and satins as much as touching something that doesn't belong rightfully to you. I may not have mentioned the specific emotion that causes temptation for you, but the result is the same. We have all experienced temptation.

> All of us also lived among them at one time, gratifying the cravings of our sinful nature and following its desires and thoughts *(Eph. 2:3).*

Scripture clearly points out that we are not to gratify ourselves when it means yielding to temptation. We are not talking about normal needs, but temptation always causes us to want more than we need. We are to be actively involved in denying this self-indulgence because temptation will not leave us alone.

> Put to death, therefore, whatever belongs to your earthly nature: sexual immorality, impurity, lust, evil desires and greed, which is idolatry *(Col. 3:5).*

> Dear friends, I urge you, as aliens and strangers in the world, to abstain from sinful desires, which war against your soul *(1 Pet. 2:11).*

> Those who belong to Christ Jesus have crucified the sinful nature with its passions and desires *(Gal. 5:24).*

It is interesting that the temptations of Jesus didn't end the first time He resisted. The fact that there were more temptations to come and that they came again so quickly lets us know that we can't let down our guard for even a minute. There will always be another temptation.

> Then the devil took him to the holy city and had him stand on the highest point of the temple. "If you are the Son of God," he said, "throw yourself down" *(Matt. 4:5-6).*

The temptations from Satan not only included indulging in pleasure but also involved the temptation of pride, to prove His position as the Son of God.

Jesus knew that when He went back to the crowds, He

would begin His ministry. He would need to convince people that He was indeed the Son of God; He wanted them to believe Him and to follow Him.

That leap from the Temple pinnacle would use sensationalism to get people to notice Him. "Look at Me," that leap would say. "See, I'm somebody special; pay attention."

It wasn't wrong for Jesus to want the people to notice Him or to believe in Him and follow Him. But using sensationalism would only appeal to the lower side of men's nature. There would have been no spiritual value in it at all.

Pride can be a disastrous thing. Unhealthy pride in who we are, in what we've achieved, what our position in the community is, and in what we possess can all be the first step to a sudden crash.

I know a young woman who spends hours preening before her mirror each day. "My looks are all I have," she told me. She is attractive, and because she is extremely attentive to her appearance, she catches attention. Her pride in herself consumes her. As she ages, eventually her outward appearance will fade, and in her eyes, she will have nothing left.

The same thing is true with pride of achievement. My mother once typed a résumé for a man that listed seven pages of achievements. These weren't just run-of-the-mill items, but as a Ph.D., he had set and achieved many difficult and extremely involved goals. He had more degrees after his name than I can recite. But no matter how much we achieve, there will always be someone else who achieves more. Someone will come along and discover something better that will cause our work, our achievements, and the memory of them to fade.

Achievement isn't enough, and neither is pride in our position. You may be a person of wealth and position in your community, but both of those things can quickly change. Your wealth may be lost in the single stroke of a pen, and your position destroyed by a false accusation. The temptation of pride, to think more of ourselves than we should, is the beginning of being dragged away and enticed by our own desires.

It isn't sinful to look nice, or to strive for achievement, or to be wealthy, or to have a prominent position in the community. But we need to be careful lest the temptations that go with those things cause us to fall away.

Perhaps your pride comes because you're the oldest daughter in the family. You think this gives you certain authority over others or that you have a right to a greater inheritance than your brothers or sisters. Or perhaps you've worked hard and have been able to amass certain special possessions. Remember that none of these things has spiritual value. Inheritances can melt into nothing, and possessions can be lost, stolen, or destroyed, so that whatever it is that causes you to be proud can cease to exist.

> If anyone thinks he is something when he is nothing, he deceives himself (Gal. 6:3).

Satan didn't give up with just two temptations of the Son of God. He added a third one. We've looked at the temptations of pleasure and pride, but there was another angle Satan wanted to try—the temptation of power.

> Again, the devil took him to a very high mountain and showed him all the kingdoms of the world and their splendor. "All of this I will give you," he said, "if you will bow down and worship me" (Matt. 4:8-9).

The same temptation comes to us. If only you'll compromise just a bit on the job, then you'll get that promotion and all the power and authority you know you deserve. Then people will pay attention to you and your ideas! If you can just get elected to the presidency of your club or to the city council, then you'll have the power to run things *your way*. Or if only you can be elected to the church board or be put in charge of the Sunday School, then you could straighten things out!

Power is a dangerous temptation. Even the disciples weren't free from that temptation. Mark records an attempt by James and John to gain power and position.

> Let one of us sit at your right and the other at your left in your glory.

Jesus answered their request by saying,

> To sit at my right or left is not for me to grant. These places belong to those for whom they have been prepared *(10:37-40)*.

There are power struggles at play every day, whether it's on the job, in the church, or in the home. The Book of James tells us why and what to do about it.

> What causes fights and quarrels among you? Don't they come from your desires that battle within you? You want something but don't get it. You kill and covet, but you cannot have what you want. You quarrel and fight. You do not have, because you do not ask God. When you ask, you do not receive, because you ask with wrong motives, that you may spend what you get on your pleasures. . . . Submit yourselves, then, to God. Resist the devil, and he will flee from you *(4:1-3, 7)*.

It isn't wrong to be a king or a supervisor or on the church board, but it is wrong to allow the power of that position to take control. Power can entice us so quickly that we won't see the evil in it until we've yielded to its temptation. Jesus saw that yielding to the temptation to gain power, even for a moment, would not bring about God's best plan. No one can serve two masters. Jesus could not serve both God and Satan.

> For everything in the world—the cravings of sinful man, the lust of his eyes and the boasting of what he has and does—comes not from the Father but from the world *(1 John 2:16)*.

As we live and grow in our spiritual walk, we can become more and more alert to temptation and learn how to avert it. One way to sidestep this kind of attack by Satan is through avoiding known areas of personal temptation.

If you know a certain thing is a temptation to you, find a way of living that will cause you to avoid that situation. Since I know that eating too much chocolate is an over-indulgence for me, I try not to have any of it in my house. If it's there, I will be strongly tempted to eat it.

If you find yourself strongly attracted to a man other than your husband, make the conscious choice not to go where that person will be. If you have to be near him, take another person with you so that you will never be alone with him.

There are a number of other things you can do in this situation. Make it a matter of honest prayer, seeking forgiveness and strength through the Holy Spirit. Sometimes a temptation is too strong to resist on your own. In those cases, seek the help and guidance of a strong Christian friend or counselor.

The more conscious we are of our areas of temptation, the better we can fight them. If it helps you to identify them more specifically, write them in your prayer diary. Choose daily—hourly, if necessary—to avoid that situation through God's strength.

Jesus didn't leave us to fight against temptation all alone. He gave us His example of not yielding, but He also allowed us to see the method He used as He resisted Satan.

There wasn't anyone watching while Jesus was being tempted. No one stood by with a video recorder or even a clay tablet to write down what Jesus said and did. But He chose to share this very intimate look into His life with us for the purpose of teaching us what to do.

When Satan offered that first temptation, Jesus quoted Scripture to turn Satan away. When the second temptation came and Satan even quoted Scripture to substantiate his position, Jesus quoted more Scripture to counter it. And, sure enough, with the third temptation, Jesus resisted by quoting still more Scripture.

> Jesus answered, "It is written: 'Man does not live on bread alone, but on every word that comes from the mouth of God'" *(Matt. 4:4)*.

> Jesus answered him, "It is also written: 'Do not put the Lord your God to the test'" *(v. 7)*.

> Jesus said to him, "Away from me, Satan! For it is written: 'Worship the Lord your God, and serve him only'" *(v. 10)*.

How can we resist temptation? First, we need to realize that Jesus understands our situation. He knows how tempting, how desirable, and how difficult our struggle is.

> Because he himself suffered when he was tempted, he is able to help those who are being tempted *(Heb. 2:18)*.

Did you understand that? It says Jesus *suffered* when He was tempted. It wasn't easy for Him to resist. There were struggles within himself in order for Him to come out victorious, or they wouldn't have been temptations. Within those three temptations Jesus suffered *everything* that any person would ever endure. He understands our suffering.

> No temptation has seized you except what is common to man. And God is faithful; he will not let you be tempted beyond what you can bear. But when you are tempted, he will also provide a way out so that you can stand up under it *(1 Cor. 10:13)*.

As soon as we recognize that our particular temptation situation is not unique, that it has been suffered before by other people and by Jesus himself, then we can better resist it. Search the Scriptures for similar situations. Write down verses that apply. Look for God's promises.

One of the ways to resist or avoid a tempting situation

is to focus on God and on the Bible. By getting our mind off the situation and onto God, we lessen the strength of the temptation. Then as we find verses that apply, we can begin quoting them. Write them on a card that you can carry with you. Glance at it throughout the day. Claim the power of God to provide victory. As we focus on God, we will begin to walk more closely to Him.

> So I say, live by the Spirit, and you will not gratify
> the desires of the sinful nature (Gal. 5:16).

When the time of temptation was over, the angels came and ministered to Jesus (Matt. 4:11). When your time of temptation ends, Jesus will minister to you. Though it isn't easy to resist temptation, it will be worth it when Jesus heals your hurts and proclaims, "Well done, thou good and faithful servant" (Matt. 25:21, KJV).

Temptation does not have to defeat us in our Christian walk. We do not have to live in a squirrel cage, constantly failing under the pressure of temptation, seeking God's forgiveness and failing once again. God helps us overcome the power of temptation, as seen from these verses in 1 John.

> My dear children, I write this to you so that you
> will not sin (2:1).

That word "will" indicates that sinning is a choice. We don't have to sin; when we allow our own desires to take control, we have made a willful choice.

But if we do sin, Jesus is our Defender:

> But if anybody does sin, we have one who speaks to
> the Father in our defense—Jesus Christ, the Righteous
> One. He is the atoning sacrifice for our sins, and not
> only for ours but also for the sins of the whole world
> (2:1-2).

Jesus paid the price of our sin with His life. When we sin, we need to claim that sacrifice. As we claim the blood of Christ's atonement, then He will forgive us.

We need to come humbly before Christ and begin with confession.

> If we confess our sins, he is faithful and just and will forgive us our sins and purify us from all unrighteousness *(1:9)*.

Confession needs to involve true contrition. It isn't enough to be sorry that we sinned; we need to be so contrite that we will not continue in that sin. We will, instead, choose to obey Christ's commands.

> We know that we have come to know him if we obey his commands *(2:3)*.

The true believer will choose to obey His commands.

> But if anyone obeys his word, God's love is truly made complete in him. This is how we know we are in him: Whoever claims to live in him must walk as Jesus did *(2:5-6)*.

If we are obeying His commands, we will not sin, for God never commands us to sin. Remembering that to be tempted is not sin; we are never left to face temptation alone. The Bible is full of promises to help us be victorious over Satan.

> Never will I leave you; never will I forsake you *(Heb. 13:5)*.

> You, dear children, are from God and have overcome them, because the one who is in you is greater than the one who is in the world *(1 John 4:4)*.

(See also Rom. 16:20; 1 Cor. 10:13; Heb. 2:18; James 4:7; and Rev. 3:10.)

Not only are we never left to face temptation and trials alone, but also we are told exactly what kind of attitude to have. We aren't to moan and groan under this kind of pressure. Instead, we are to be consumed with joy:

> Dear friends, do not be surprised at the painful trial you are suffering, as though something strange were

happening to you. But rejoice that you participate in the
sufferings of Christ, so that you may be overjoyed when
his glory is revealed *(1 Pet. 4:12-13).*

Facing temptation and overcoming it is part of the maturing process for Christians. This is one of many growth
methods God allows in our lives to help us become holy
women. When we can face temptation and trials with joy,
we know we are reacting as Christ would, though in reality,
it is Christ within us who reacts with joy.

God promises us a crown of life if we withstand this
kind of testing.

Blessed is the man who perseveres under trial, because when he has stood the test, he will receive the
crown of life that God has promised to those who love
him *(James 1:12).*

One of the greatest defense mechanisms we have in
countering Satan's attacks is a system of accountability.
Think of the word *accountable* as being a lifeline. Stretch the
first segment of this lifeline between yourself and God, and
the second segment between yourself and at least one other
Christian. Together, those two segments of the lifeline will
hold us firmly if our feet stumble.

God wants us to be accountable to Him. From Genesis
to Revelation, He has made it clear that we are to follow His
commands, or there are serious consequences. In other
words, He is constantly aware of every one of us. We need to
turn that awareness around and be conscious of Him. Just
knowing that He is aware of us will make us stop and
think about what we are doing.

Scripture says:

Whoever claims to live in him must walk as Jesus
did *(1 John 2:6).*

Obedience to His Word and following His example is
our portion of the commitment to be accountable to God.
When we bow before Him in prayer, we invite Him to show

us any error of our ways so that we can conform to His will. King David prayed:

> Search me, O God, and know my heart; test me and know my anxious thoughts. See if there is any offensive way in me, and lead me in the way everlasting *(Ps. 139:23-24).*

The other half of the lifeline is being accountable to other Christians. The well-known advertising jingle "Reach out and touch someone" is valid in the spiritual realm too. If everyone who is a Christian reached out and grasped firmly the hand of one other Christian, we would keep each other from stumbling. One of our major jobs is helping one another keep focused on Christ.

I have a very special Christian friend with whom I share a mutual agreement. If either of us sees the other making a choice that would turn us away from Christ, we immediately confront the other. In love, we point out the error and pray with one another.

> My brothers, if one of you should wander from the truth and someone should bring him back, remember this: Whoever turns a sinner from the error of his way will save him from death and cover over a multitude of sins *(James 5:19-20).*

> Therefore confess your sins to each other and pray for each other so that you may be healed. The prayer of a righteous man is powerful and effective *(v. 16).*

The person you choose to whom you will be accountable should be a mature Christian whose life-style clearly shows a close walk with God. That person should be one who knows how to keep a confidence (and so should you!) and still be willing to confront you in the love of Christ. This needs to be someone who is generally a part of your everyday world. If she is too far removed from you physically, she may not detect a subtle change in your life quickly enough to keep you from falling. The shorter the rope, the less you will stray from the path.

Do Christians experience temptation? Yes!

Do they have to yield? No!

* * *

THINK ON THESE THINGS

1. List (for your eyes alone) some areas of temptation in your life that God is showing you today.

2. Find a verse of Scripture related to each one that will help you resist that temptation.

3. What do you plan to do to avoid these areas, now that you've clearly identified them?

4. Discuss with several other people the difference between having nice possessions and yielding to the temptation they could bring.

5. How can you help other people who may be going through a time of temptation?

6. In what way can you make yourself accountable to God?

7. Name at least one person to whom you will make yourself accountable, and set up a date and time to get together for accountability and prayer.

* * *

Books to read:

Temptation, Charles Stanley
Seven Deadly Sins, Anthony Campolo

8

Stress and the Holy Woman

"I can't take it anymore!" Tears filled Wendy's eyes. *"I have a meeting every night this week, a Bible study class to prepare for Thursday morning, and Bill is out of town, so I have his mother to check on while he's gone. On top of that the choir director moved, and the church wants me to fill in until they can hire someone. Then I'm room mother for Janie's third grade class, so I have to be at the school every afternoon."*

Her voice trembled as she continued. "With Bill's dad in the nursing home, it looks as if I'll have to get a job to help with expenses too!" Her hands shook as she fumbled for a tissue. "It just doesn't seem to end. I don't have time for devotions much anymore, and my prayer life consists of 'God bless this mess!'" She sighed heavily. "Just where is God in all this anyway?"

Wendy sounds like a lot of women I know. We live in a stress-filled society. Is it possible to be holy under all that stress?

At whatever stage we are in life, there are pressures that can and will rob us of our private communion with Christ. We may find we are so tired from all the stress that we sleep right through the morning alarm and miss our quiet time. By the time we wake up, there is only enough time to prepare for work or our first appointment.

"God understands my schedule," we might use for an excuse. "If He wants me to have a quiet time with Him, He'll have to create the extra minutes in my day." Sometimes it seems impossible to even think about God in the middle of our busyness. When we are in the midst of chaos, holiness seems far away—and so does God. We may think God doesn't really care. The Israelites felt that way too.

> Why do you say, O Jacob, and complain, O Israel, "My way is hidden from the Lord; my cause is disregarded by my God"? *(Isa. 40:27)*.

But Isaiah helped them turn their eyes away from their difficulties and focus on God. They needed to remember how much God loved them and cared about them, and so do we.

> He gives strength to the weary and increases the power of the weak *(v. 29)*.
>
> I will strengthen you and help you; I will uphold you with my righteous right hand *(41:10)*.

In order to cope with stress in our world, we need to rely on the strength that comes through a solid relationship with Christ. It is the power of the Holy Spirit within us that makes it possible to survive in our stress-filled society. In the eye of the hurricane, there is a place of quietness. It doesn't change the fact that there's a storm raging; but when we turn control of the storm over to God, there is calm in the middle of the chaos.

The question arises: Does stress cause a diminishing in our relationship with Christ, or does some lack in our spiritual condition cause increasing stress? Or is stress even related to our spiritual condition?

Most of us think that if we do a lot of work for God, it indicates a greater level of spirituality. The truth is, we often take on more than we can handle, never asking God how much we should be doing. In this way we create our own stress. God does not give us greater burdens than we can bear. But sometimes through our own choices we add pounds to our burden that God never intended in the first place.

In this sense, stress is related to our failure to seek God's guidance. However, there are stresses in our lives over which we have no control: deaths, marriages, births, illness, job changes, finances, etc. These bring stresses to the greatest saint and are not a result of our choices.

Stress can be placed on us by other people. Several pastors that I know are nursing ulcers due to pressures and stress brought on by obstinate church board members. Office and other workers labor under heavy stress caused by demands made in an executive board meeting or by a supervisor who increases their work load. Stress can be caused when family members don't carry their part of the load. Anytime people are inconsiderate of others, it produces stress. The Bible offers guidelines that would prevent this kind of stress:

> Make sure that nobody pays back wrong for wrong, but always try to be kind to each other and to everyone else *(1 Thess. 5:15)*.

Most Christian women are overinvolved. This produces stress. We tell ourselves that we can never do enough when it comes to God's work, and we deny that we are doing too much. But denying stress only lets it build up like steam in a pressure cooker. Sooner or later it's going to blow!

Denial turns our stress inward and can cause depression. We think horribly depressing thoughts and then chastise ourselves, feeling we are denying the power of God and have therefore sinned.

Depression is an emotion, not a choice of the will. No one wants to be depressed. For that matter, no one wants to be overstressed, either. Both stress and depression are a *result* of something else, not a cause.

There will be times when we won't feel holy. Sometimes stress will cause us to experience emotional lows. The same thing can happen when we are ill or sad. Do our emotions affect our relationship to God? Are we more spiritual when we are happy than when we aren't? Emotional highs don't make us more holy, nor do they prove our state of holiness. The Holy Spirit sanctifies us through faith:

> So that they may receive forgiveness of sins and a place among those who are sanctified by faith in me (Acts 26:18).

Our relationship with God is based on faith in God's promises. Emotions are a by-product of the moment and can never be used as a thermometer of our relationship to God.

How we feel doesn't matter nearly so much as what our commitment is. It takes an act of the will to exercise faith and make a commitment to God. Emotions, if they enter into our relationship with God at all, are a side effect.

Christian workers, whether they are pastors, missionaries, or other full-time workers, often succumb to stress caused by fatigue or illness. We need to be alert to stress symptoms in those who are in full-time Christian service. When stress is caused by physical factors, the best treatment is rest and restoration. This may involve counseling and assistance from people close to us, as well as medical help.

This past year, I have several times talked or prayed with missionary friends who are experiencing stress symptoms. In each case, these dear ones had not taken time to relax for many months, even years. They have carried the weight of the missionary work on their shoulders, knowing how much work needed to be done and never being able to do it all.

Many of us fall into the trap of trying to "do it all." The truth is, we can't. Jesus couldn't when He was on this earth. He could only work in a small area and with a few men. He poured himself out, but He also knew when it was time to withdraw and be restored.

We are no less holy when we take time to rest and be restored than when we are working at our God-assigned tasks at a feverish pace. The work we do after we have rested produces quality fruit in those around us.

> A cheerful heart is good medicine, but a crushed spirit dries up the bones *(Prov. 17:22)*.

What do we do when our world crashes around us and the worst we feared actually happens? When a teenage daughter runs away from home, pregnant and on drugs, or when a precious son's life is snuffed out when he was only beginning to blossom, where does holiness fit?

Most of us aren't thinking about holiness when we are dangling at the end of our rope! Our hands are numb from holding on, and we're dizzy from the gale-force winds that are battering us. Generally, at this point we are screaming, "Where are You, God?"

My grandson decided to climb to the top of the jungle gym at the park and suddenly discovered he was too far from the ground for comfort. "Grandma, I'm falling!" he yelled. Hanging by his fingertips, he was only inches from my grasp.

"Let go, I'll catch you," I called. But his eyes were shut tight as he expected to crash to the ground, and he continued to cling fast to the top bar. When he thought the worst was happening, his grasp slipped, and he dropped easily into my waiting arms. He was more shocked that I caught him than he would have been had he hit the ground.

When we are at the end of our rope, Jesus has provided an incredible holding power—praise! Praising God over and over will lift us and remind us who He is. It may not be possible to praise God *for* the situation we are in, but we can praise Him *while we are in it.*

There is power in the name of Jesus. Even though it may seem difficult, we are commanded to praise God perpetually:

> Through Jesus, therefore, let us continually offer to

God a sacrifice of praise—the fruit of lips that confess his name *(Heb. 13:15)*.

In this you greatly rejoice, though now for a little while you may have had to suffer grief in all kinds of trials *(1 Pet. 1:6)*.

Eternity is worth all that we're going through now. It is the praise we give to God in each situation that gives us hope. We don't have to live defeated, stressed out, or in despair. Hope in Christ lifts us up. Praise is the holy way, the higher way to live.

There is a ladder by which we can climb out of the pit caused by stress and reach spiritual strength.

Consider it pure joy, my brothers, whenever you face trials of many kinds, because you know that the testing of your faith develops perseverance. Perseverance must finish its work so that you may be mature and complete, not lacking anything *(James 1:2-4)*.

Note that there are five steps on God's stress ladder:
1. Trials—produce testing of your faith.
2. Testing—of your faith brings perseverance.
3. Perseverance—produces maturity.
4. Maturity—is completeness, not lacking in anything.
5. Joy gives strength—the joy of the Lord is my strength.

We don't start with "joy." That's the top rung of the ladder. Instead, we start right where we are in the middle of our trials, bombed out by stress. It's here in the struggles of our day-to-day living that the testing of our faith occurs.

There are numerous examples in the Bible of people under stress. Here are a few, and all of them started right where we are, slugging it out in the trenches, enduring trials. Consider:

Jesus, John the Baptist, Mary and Joseph, Peter, Paul, King David, Elijah, King Saul, Moses, Abraham, Ruth, Esther, Caleb

Each of them experienced trials and stresses that were

unique from any other person's problems. Most of them chose as a rule to turn to God for their strength, though at least one did not. None of them, except Jesus, was perfect.

It's the testing times of our faith that bring perseverance. Elijah was a strong man of faith (read 1 Kings 17—18). He had an intimate relationship with God that transcended even the natural laws of earth. When the widow's son died (17:17-24), Elijah prayed and God restored life to the young boy. Earlier when he needed to prove God's power, Elijah prayed and God withheld rain from the earth:

> Now Elijah the Tishbite, from Tishbe in Gilead, said to Ahab, "As the Lord, the God of Israel, lives, whom I serve, there will be neither dew nor rain in the next few years except at my word" *(v. 1)*

Elijah, the man of faith, confronted a king with his sin, defeated a passel of false prophets, and called down fire from heaven (18:38). Then he prayed again, and rain fell in torrents after a period of 3½ years of drought. Nothing should be able to defeat this kind of man, right? But under stress, things changed.

Just three short verses after such tremendous victory, in the 19th chapter of 1 Kings, we find some very strange words:

> Elijah was afraid and ran for his life *(v. 3)*.
> [He sat under a tree] and prayed that he might die. "I have had enough, Lord," he said. "Take my life; I am no better than my ancestors." Then he lay down under the tree and fell asleep *(vv. 4-5)*.

Elijah, the man of faith, became Elijah, a man in despair. He was afraid and ran for his life; he wanted to die. What happened to change this man of such towering spiritual strength?

First, he was physically exhausted and emotionally drained. He had poured himself out before God and man, giving everything he had in full measure—and adding a bit more. There were no reserves left. When the battle was over, a tremendous letdown (both physical and spiritual) occurred.

It is normal for us to experience this kind of letdown after heavy physical, emotional, and spiritual battles. At this low ebb we, like Elijah, can be vulnerable to the tiniest prick of the enemy's sword. Just one more jab—a threat by a woman to kill him just as he had killed the false prophets —and Elijah slid nonstop to the end of his rope.

> So Jezebel sent a messenger to Elijah to say, "May the gods deal with me, be it ever so severely, if by this time tomorrow I do not make your life like that of one of them" *(1 Kings 19:2)*.

How did God handle Elijah's problem? The first thing He did was to give Elijah some physical rest. Elijah slept. Then He provided physical food. It's interesting to note that Elijah was fed by His messenger. I wonder how many times He has fed us by the hands of His messengers, and we never realized who they were.

> All at once an angel touched him and said, "Get up and eat." He looked around, and there by his head was a cake of bread baked over hot coals, and a jar of water. He ate and drank and then lay down again *(vv. 5-6)*.

God not only fed him once but also fed him again (vv. 7-8). Then Elijah traveled out of the desert to the mountain of God (Horeb), where he went into a cave. Here we find he is virtually reborn in spirit as God meets with him in the morning. When his body was strengthened, he was confronted by God and spiritually restored.

Elijah, man of faith who became a man of fear and depression, is now a man of strength. When he was physically refreshed and spiritually restored, he went on to more work for God, doing what He commanded him to do (vv. 15-19, etc.).

Elijah did not stay defeated. God allowed him to return

to his called area of service. What a great example for us of His gracious restoring power. It's so easy to stay down in the muck, wallowing in defeat. Or once the battle is over, to remove ourselves from the fight. But God calls us back to service.

It's the cycle of trials-testing-persevering that teaches us one of our most valuable lessons. God is faithful! If He has called you to complete a specific task, He will be faithful to you. When we have poured out all we have, He will be faithful to restore us. No matter how fierce the battle or how exhausted we get, His strength is never depleted; there is always more than enough!

Nowhere in the Bible does it say the Holy Spirit ever gave up the battle. When He empowers us, His infinite strength is more than enough for us to persevere, no matter how many battles we fight.

As we cycle through the trials, testing, and persevering, learning God's great lessons, we naturally move one more step up the ladder to maturity. An untested, immature Christian does not yet know that God's strength is sufficient to meet all our needs. But when we've been through battle after battle, experience produces maturity and intimate knowledge of God in action.

Age does not necessarily mean maturity. It is experience that makes the difference and produces maturity.

In the Old Testament, Caleb was a man who had experienced God in action. He knew what life had been like in Egypt and had experienced God's wonderful deliverance. He had seen the Red Sea become a dry path. He knew what God could do. When the time came for him to explore the Promised Land, he viewed it through eyes of maturity.

> We should go up and take possession of the land, for we can certainly do it *(Num. 13:30).*

> If the Lord is pleased with us, he will lead us into

that land . . . the Lord is with us. Do not be afraid
(14:8-9).

God was faithful to Caleb, and at 85 years of age he was
still strong in his faith.

> I was forty years old when Moses the servant of the
> Lord sent me from Kadesh Barnea to explore the land.
> . . . So here I am today, eighty-five years old! I am still as
> strong today as the day Moses sent me out; I'm just as
> vigorous to go out to battle now as I was then *(Josh. 14:7,
> 10-11)*.

When it comes to God's strength, our physical age has
nothing to do with it. The progress from stress to maturity
is based on our relationship and experience with God. We
may feel fairly secure when we find ourselves this high on
the ladder, but there is still one more step.

Let us read this passage in James closely. He begins it by
saying: "Consider it pure joy, my brothers [and sisters],
whenever you face trials." The last rung on the ladder, the
one that takes us all the way to the top, is step number five,
JOY.

How do we get this joy? We set our minds on joy. Notice
James doesn't say "if" you face trials, he tells us to actually
expect trials. And then he tells us what our attitude should
be. We are to "consider it pure joy." Every time we find ourselves going through some type of trial, we need to remind
ourselves that it will bring us all to the top of the ladder.
That makes the trial worthwhile and gives us an overall
perspective, which allows us to have an attitude of joy.

Are you in a trial right now? Begin with prayer. Joy
comes to us while we are praying.

> I will . . . give them joy in my house of prayer *(Isa.
> 56:7)*.

Songs about our Lord are a great source of joy. As we
sing to Him and about Him, we are reminded of who He is.

We remember that He is the Victor, He is our Strength, He is our Redeemer.

> Sing for joy to God our strength *(Ps. 81:1)*.

When we are in the very depths of our trials, we can make a deliberate choice that will help not only ourselves but also others. Smile! Relaxing our face muscles will ease our own tension. It may shock us when we walk past a mirror and find a smiling face looking back at us, but it works.

> A cheerful look brings joy to the heart *(Prov. 15:30)*.

When stress seems to be overwhelming us, we are to strengthen ourselves in the Lord. This deliberate choice to climb one rung higher is where the real strength comes from.

> Do not grieve, for the joy of the Lord is your strength *(Neh. 8:10)*.

And finally, we are to turn the whole situation over to God, placing our full trust in the Lord.

> May the God of hope fill you with all joy and peace as you trust in him, so that you may overflow with hope by the power of the Holy Spirit *(Rom. 15:13)*.

Our hope in Christ is the glue that holds us together when our world is crumbling around us.

> Therefore, strengthen your feeble arms and weak knees. "Make level paths for your feet," so that the lame may not be disabled, but rather healed *(Heb. 12:12-13)*.

Are your knees weak? Are your arms feeble? Do you feel spiritually disabled?

Are you part of God's walking wounded? Then read again some of the wonderful promises in the Bible that are ours to claim:

> The Lord upholds all those who fall and lifts up all who are bowed down *(Ps. 145:14)*.

The Lord is my rock, my fortress and my deliverer; my God is my rock, in whom I take refuge. He is my shield and the horn of my salvation, my stronghold *(18:2)*.

My flesh and my heart may fail, but God is the strength of my heart and my portion forever *(73:26)*.

He gives strength to the weary and increases the power of the weak. . . . those who hope in the Lord will renew their strength. They will soar on wings like eagles; they will run and not grow weary, they will walk and not be faint *(Isa. 40:29, 31)*.

I can do everything through him who gives me strength *(Phil. 4:13)*.

* * *

Think on These Things

1. What is causing stress in your life right now?

2. How can you change your situation to help combat that stress through rest, relaxation, medical attention, or counseling, etc.?

3. In what way have you been relying on your emotions to be your thermometer for measuring your relationship with God?

4. In what way can you change your spiritual circumstances to help you combat stress?

5. Are you honestly experiencing the joy of the Lord in your current circumstances? If not, what do you plan to do about it?

6. Name someone other than yourself who is going through a time of stress. What can you do this week to be God's messenger to that person to provide strength, encouragement, and rest?

7. Read the 17th chapter of John. Find out:
    1. What protects us (vv. 11-12)
    2. How much joy we should have (v. 13)
    3. Where we are being sent (v. 18)
    4. Why we are being sent there (v. 23)
    5. Whose love dwells in us (v. 26)

                    *   *   *

Books to read:

Regaining Control of Your Life, Judson Edwards
Women Under Stress, Randy and Nanci Alcorn
Stress Fractures, Charles Swindoll
Waiting on God, Andrew Murray
Guaranteed Steps to Managing Stress, Arnold Burron and
    Jerry Crews

9

Holiness in the Workplace

"There is absolutely no way to be a Christian in my job." Tami shook her head violently. "My boss cheats on his income tax—that's stealing; he promises deliveries to customers that he knows will be late—that's lying! The off-color jokes and swearwords used daily would turn the air blue. There are under-the-table deals that never get entered in the books, and I'm told to keep my mouth shut about them." Tami shoved her hands into her pockets, fists clenched tightly. "For sure Jesus wouldn't feel comfortable working there. I don't know how He expects me to act like a Christian—it just isn't possible."

It would be a blessing if all of us could work in a place where everyone was a Christian. But many of us find ourselves the only Christian on the job. "Could Jesus sit at *my* desk?" is a question many people ask. Or "Could Jesus drive my truck, stand at my cash register, wait on my customers, etc.?"

Is it possible to be holy in today's workplace? It is easy to be holy on Sunday and put our Christianity away for the rest of the week. But our walk and life with Christ is to be consistent, as strong on Monday as it is on Sunday. Jesus said:

> If anyone would come after me, he must deny himself and take up his cross daily and follow me *(Luke 9:23)*.

The first thing to notice is that whatever we do, we are

to do it *daily.* The next is that we are to *follow* Christ. We don't blunder ahead of Him, we follow.

Christ's example for us to follow begins with consistency. He never lowered His standards regardless of who He was with or where He went. We need to be consistent and set our standard of conduct in the workplace so that we do not compromise our faith.

How you act, what you say, your attitude, and even the way you dress all tell about your faith in Christ far more than any preaching you might try to do.

Ladies, be sure the way you dress in the workplace reflects the holiness of Christ. I'm not about to tell you how long your skirt should be, how many buttons you can leave undone, or exactly how tight your slacks can be. But remember that we want to attract our coworkers to Christ and not focus their attention on our bodies. If a male coworker is having trouble keeping his eyes off you, he isn't thinking about what a great Christian you are!

Take a good look at your workspace. What message does it convey to those around you? Ask God to show you what, if anything, you can change that would bring a gentle atmosphere of holiness into that spot. Maybe you can replace a cartoon with a bit of scripture or a Christian plaque.

The people around you may not understand why you hold up the standards of Christ. They didn't understand Christ, so why would *you* be understood?

> If the world hates you, keep in mind that it hated me first. If you belonged to the world, it would love you as its own. As it is, you do not belong to the world, but I have chosen you out of the world. That is why the world hates you *(John 15:18-19).*

Because they don't understand, they may sneer or even deliberately cause you difficulty on the job. No matter how they treat you, you are to hold fast to Christ's standards in a gentle, loving, but firm manner. Let Jesus shine through you so that others can find Him.

It was my first day in a new office. This was a promotion I'd wanted for a long time. There were four desks crammed into a tiny room, two bosses each with his secretary.

I dreaded this first day because I knew that one of the men from the plant came to that office to deliver the morning stat sheets. It was his habit—even his joy—to have a new joke every day. I had heard some of them, and they were definitely off-color. Armed with prayer, I waited for his arrival.

Sure enough, he came and dropped the papers on my desk. Then in a loud voice he delivered his daily joke. He was aware of my stand as a Christian, so he chose a religious story that was only slightly off-color. Then he waited for my reaction. So did my coworkers.

With a sudden insight from God, I looked at him with a deadpan face, thanked him for delivering the papers, and turned back to my job without further comment. When he left the room, my boss turned to me and said very quietly, "Thank you for not responding to him. I've never liked his jokes but didn't want to say anything. If we don't encourage him by laughing, I think the jokes will stop."

The message must have filtered back to him through the grapevine, because he never told another off-color joke in my presence. But because I didn't put him down or make any demands that he stop, there was no animosity between us.

I decided at that time that I didn't have to listen to jokes of that nature. If someone starts a story that I know will be off-color, I quietly move away until they are finished. If I must remain within hearing distance, I do not laugh or even acknowledge what was said. My rule of thumb is: don't listen, don't laugh, don't lend credence to it.

If you act in this manner, it won't be long before someone will ask, "Why do you do that?" If the question is asked, you have every right to answer it. This is the opening you need to tell them about your faith in Christ. It's also a time to reassure them that Christians can have fun; but they have clean fun. As long as we respond with the love of Christ, we will gain the respect of those around us. They may not agree with us, but if our stand is consistent, they'll respect us.

Sometimes a boss or coworker, or even certain customers, are difficult to work with. Maybe they don't do their share of the job, or they are continually late to work. They might be always complaining or faultfinding. People like that make our workdays seem longer and more tiring, taking the joy out of a job that could be fun.

How can a Christian handle these people? The same way Christ would. In fact, that's what we need to do as we meet the people who fill our day. How would Christ handle them?

First of all, Jesus loves them!

> For God so loved the world that he gave his one and only Son, that whoever believes in him shall not perish but have eternal life. For God did not send his Son into the world to condemn the world, but to save the world through him *(John 3:16-17)*.

Jesus loves those difficult people—so much that He died for them. Because He loves them that much, He would treat them in love. This may be part of that daily cross we must bear, but we are to follow Jesus' example and love them, even if they treat us poorly.

> But I tell you who hear me: Love your enemies, do good to those who hate you, bless those who curse you, pray for those who mistreat you *(Luke 6:27-28)*.

It is difficult to respond lovingly and calmly to someone who is pounding on your desk, screaming in red-faced rage. But Christ *in* us can love them *through* us if we allow Him control.

There is a scriptural strategy that can be implemented to help you live a holy life in an unholy workplace. Whether the problem is that you have been asked to do something wrong, or it's an ongoing problem that must be dealt with daily, there is an answer that works.

We do not want the enemy to defeat us in this highly visible part of our lives. The best defense is an active offense. The apostle Paul tells us how to begin.

> Finally, be strong in the Lord and in his mighty power. Put on the full armor of God so that you can take your stand against the devil's schemes. For our struggle is not against flesh and blood, but against the rulers, against the authorities, against the powers of this dark world and against the spiritual forces of evil in the heavenly realms. Therefore put on the full armor of God, so that when the day of evil comes, you may be able to stand your ground, and after you have done everything, to stand. Stand firm then, with the belt of truth buckled around your waist, with the breastplate of righteousness in place, and with your feet fitted with the readiness that comes from the gospel of peace. In addition to all this, take up the shield of faith, with which you can extinguish all the flaming arrows of the evil one. Take the helmet of salvation and the sword of the Spirit, which is the word of God. And pray in the Spirit on all occasions with all kinds of prayers and requests *(Eph. 6:10-18)*.

This strategy is simple: Be right with God; be ready for the enemy. Begin your preparation daily by making sure everything is right between you and God through reading the Bible and communing with Him in prayer. Submit yourself to God so that you are part of the solution, not part of the problem.

Pray that the presence of God will be evident in your

workplace. Ask God to fill your workspace with himself just as though He were filling the Old Testament Temple! Pray about your attitude toward the people who will come in contact with you during the day. Pray for the right words to speak to them, for the right answer for decisions you must make. Pray, pray, pray!

Then use the Sword of the Spirit, the Word of God, to slice through the enemy. If you can, keep some appropriate Scripture verses near you throughout the day. When your eyes catch sight of Bible verses, your mind automatically turns to God. Constantly and consistently memorize Bible verses.

When a difficult situation arises, pause momentarily before responding. During that pause, mentally quote a portion of the Bible. It will slow down that instantaneous retort that might not be in keeping with a Christlike attitude, and it may change the way you think about the situation. Pray before you speak and while you are speaking. It's wonderful how God has made it possible for us to communicate with Him at the same time we are doing other things! In this workplace war, we need to do whatever is necessary to keep the enemy from defeating us.

But what if *home* is your workplace, as mine now is? Is this any different from working outside of the home? Let's be honest; it's sometimes very difficult to think about being holy women when the kids are screaming, supper is burning, and the checkbook won't balance.

Because we have a family business that operates out of our home, my office is located in a corner of my kitchen. Having worked both outside and in the home, I find little difference. I have pressures of year-end bookkeeping, a computer that hiccups, and customers who can be very difficult. I also have to remember that Jesus loves the people who call me to chat because they think I'm not busy or doing anything that's important because I'm at home!

Whether your job is raising a family and managing a home or working in the business world, holiness doesn't change. Dealing with a difficult child (spouse, parent, etc.) is the same as dealing with a difficult customer. We have to ask the same question, "How would Jesus handle this person?"

Use the same holy strategy for your home as for the office. Be right with God; be ready for the enemy. And, above all, pray. Ask God to fill those walls with His holy presence from floor to ceiling, from basement to attic.

Is your checkbook committed to Christ? Just as you wouldn't expect a Christian businessman to steal, neither should you write checks that you know will bounce! A businessman needs to work on a budget, and so do you. If your checkbook and budget are a disaster, bring them to God through prayer for His guidance and control. Allow Him to bring order out of chaos. Seek financial counseling if it's needed. It's a bit difficult to witness to the bank teller while she's explaining that your account is overdrawn!

When we allow the Holy Spirit to control our lives, the world in which we live becomes a better place. The circumstances don't necessarily change, but *we* change, conforming to Christ, bringing Him into our everyday world. The Holy Spirit in us will bring order out of chaos, joy out of disaster. When we allow Him to work in us and through us, there will be visible results—wherever we work!

As I said, the circumstances may not change, but our attitude and our view of the situation will change. We can ask ourselves, Is this adversity or is it an opportunity to serve Christ? In fact, a truth we sometimes overlook is that circumstances create opportunities for Christ.

Sometimes God uses negative circumstances in our jobs to force us into places where He can use us, places we wouldn't ordinarily go. Philip was in just that kind of situation. He had been selected as one of the special helpers to assist the apostles in Jerusalem. Suddenly, one of the other helpers was stoned to death, and the Jerusalem church was thrown into instant chaos. It wasn't safe to walk the streets, meet together in church, or even remain hidden in their own homes. Christians were being persecuted, dragged out of their homes, and put into prison.

So, Philip, along with all the other Christians except the apostles, left Jerusalem. He made his way to a city in Samaria and began preaching about Christ there. These were people he would never ordinarily have sought out to tell about Jesus. But the Holy Spirit knew who needed to hear the message, and the results were far beyond anything Philip imagined. Evil spirits came out of many, paralytics and cripples were healed, and the crowds paid close attention to what he said. Acts 8:8 says, "So there was great joy in that city." What an understatement! Joy because of chaos, praise because of persecution.

Philip could have hidden himself away and quietly waited for the persecution to end so that he could go back home. But he didn't. He looked for opportunities to do the work God had called him to do.

Apparently Philip was a man who listened to the voice of the Holy Spirit, because God gave him another unique opportunity.

> Now an angel of the Lord said to Philip, "Go south to the road—the desert road—that goes down from Jerusalem to Gaza" *(Acts 8:26)*.

Philip didn't hesitate. The angel said, "Go," and the next verse says, "So he started out." He didn't ask what he was supposed to do; he just obeyed. As he went along, he noticed a chariot with an Ethiopian in it. Again, the leadership of the Holy Spirit moved Philip into a unique area of ministry. The Spirit told Philip, "Go to that chariot and stay near it."

I like what happens next. "Then Philip ran." Do you *run* to do the Spirit's bidding in your workplace? So many of us drag our feet: "Lord, I don't want to do that!" We whimper and complain that God expects too much of us. "Who me? You've got to be kidding, Lord! These are my coworkers." We think up every possible excuse, but the Spirit still whispers, "Go." Next time you hear God's voice pointing out a new opportunity of ministry, try *running* to do it. See what the results are!

Philip must have been in pretty good condition to keep up to the pace of the chariot. Can't you just picture them: a horse-drawn chariot and Philip keeping perfect time as they raced down the road.

Following the leading of the Holy Spirit, Philip was able to share the gospel with the Ethiopian.

Philip wasn't there by accident. He was in exactly the spot God wanted him to be in at exactly the moment someone needed spiritual help. If he had dragged his feet instead of running, or if back in Samaria he had said, "No, I'm not going. I've got a good ministry right here," then all of Ethiopia would have missed the gospel message. Secular history tells us that Ethiopia was virtually a Christian nation for many years, and it seems to be traced back to this Ethiopian who served under the queen, Candace.

Sometimes the enormity of what we are doing simply overwhelms us. If God had said, "Philip, the whole nation of Ethiopia needs to be told about the salvation message," Philip might have figured he was only one man, Ethiopia was a big country, and there was no way he could get the job done. But the Holy Spirit knew exactly what was needed. Just one man explaining the gospel to one other man. Now that wasn't overwhelming at all.

"What can just one person do?" is an excuse that just doesn't cut it with God at all. Just one person listening to the leadership of the Holy Spirit can accomplish great things in the workplace and in the world. The results are in God's hands.

In fact, Philip barely got to see the Ethiopian come up out of the baptismal waters. That was all he ever knew of his obedience in the whole incident. There wasn't even time for a hug or some final instructions, because the Holy Spirit had another ministry to perform through Philip that required his immediate attention.

The Spirit of the Lord suddenly took Philip away, and Philip found himself in a completely different set of circumstances.

> Philip, however, appeared at Azotus and traveled about, preaching the gospel in all the towns until he reached Caesarea *(v. 40)*.

This time we aren't even told the results of Philip's preaching, but it must have been very important.

The first time Philip left Jerusalem he was forced into a new area of ministry because of chaotic, negative situations. The next ministry was a result of his obedient choice, but this third time it's just plain circumstances. The Holy Spirit knows who needs to hear the message and who doesn't. He knows where we should be and where we shouldn't be. Acts 16:6 says of Paul,

> Having been kept by the Holy Spirit from preaching the word in the province of Asia.

God expects us to minister in whatever situation we find ourselves. Have you suddenly found yourself in a new situation on your job through no fault of your own? Perhaps your boss just told you he's having to close down your department, and there isn't any place in the company for you. It isn't your fault; it just happened.

Are you going to huddle in a corner? Maybe you've been quietly waiting for things to change, for the chaos to end or the problem to go away. Why not bloom where you are planted? Look around you for opportunities to minister instead of focusing on the adversity. Ask the Holy Spirit to show you what you can do.

The Bible reminds us that we are called to serve God, that there is work to do.

> The Holy Spirit said, "Set apart for me Barnabas and Saul for the work to which I have called them" *(Acts 13:2)*.

It isn't the job but the attitude of holiness, being led by the Holy Spirit, that makes the difference.

*   *   *

THINK ON THESE THINGS

1. As you begin your "holy strategy," what do you plan to pray about for your workplace today?

2. How can you begin showing the love of Christ to that difficult person in your life?

3. How can you change your workspace to reflect the presence of Christ?

4. What attitudes about your working situation need to be brought in prayer to Christ?

5. All of us do at least some kind of work in our homes. What can you change that will enhance the attitude and reality of holiness in your home?

6. What Scripture verses are you memorizing this week?

7. What opportunities of witnessing and ministering for Christ can you identify in your current circumstances?

*   *   *

Books to read:

The Pursuit of God, A. W. Tozer
The Deeper Christian Life, Andrew Murray

10

Trophies for the Winner

"I could be a holy person if only things were different," Helen lamented. "God can't expect me to be holy the way things are in my life right now. I have accepted Christ's forgiveness for my sins," she affirmed, "and I love God very much. But to be holy . . ." She shrugged her shoulders and let the sentence dangle. "I mean, it would take God himself to be holy in my situation."

Without realizing it, Helen stated the absolute truth. None of us can be holy; only God can be holy. But it is when we allow God to be holy *in* us that the holiness we seek becomes reality.

After salvation and we have learned to live with forgiveness, there will come a time when we will want *more* of Christ. The desire to live as He lived, to become as He was, will deepen. When that desire has grown fully and we lay our total self at the feet of Christ, then He will take control.

Holiness is an inner decision we make out of love for God. Having made that decision and having been filled with God in the person of the Holy Spirit, the holiness we seek in our lives will become a daily reality.

It is not our circumstances that determine our holiness. It's the holiness of God within us that allows us to live a holy life right now, no matter what our circumstances are.

The author of Hebrews challenges each one of us to live the holy life just as though it were a race.

Let us run with perseverance the race marked out

for us. Let us fix our eyes on Jesus, the author and per-
fecter of our faith *(12:1-2)*.

We are to focus our eyes on Jesus, not on situations or
circumstances around us. In a race, the runner needs to focus on the goal. In our daily lives, Jesus is our goal. He, and
He alone, is to be our focus.

This scripture says that we are surrounded by a cloud of
witnesses:

> Therefore, since we are surrounded by such a great
> cloud of witnesses, let us throw off everything that hin-
> ders and the sin that so easily entangles *(v. 1)*.

This verse comes at the end of a long list of people who
had their own spiritual struggles: people like Abraham,
Moses, Samuel, David, and a host of others. The picture we
are given in this chapter is like that of a Roman marathon
race. Imagine that we are in a great Roman coliseum,
dressed in Olympic-approved running gear right down to
the best racing shoes. It's not how fast we run this race, but
rather how *well* we run it that counts. The grandstands are
filled with people who have already completed their own
marathon, and now they watch to see how well each of us
will run.

Anything that keeps your focus diverted from Jesus
will trip you up as you run the race. Take a long look at
your life. What sin entangles you? Forsake it before it dam-
ages your witness for Christ.

Running a race isn't just *beginning* well. It also involves
endurance. Racers tell me that in a long race they soon lose
sight of all that is around them and focus only on running.
Putting one foot in front of the other, lap after lap, around
the track takes all their attention. Endurance, then, is the
next important function after beginning.

The Bible says we are to keep on running our race for
Christ.

> Let us not become weary in doing good, for at the
> proper time we will reap a harvest if we do not give up
> *(Gal. 6:9).*

Endurance is holiness in action. When we keep on living the holy life day after day (putting one foot in front of the other, lap after lap around the track), we will eventually reap the harvest of our labors.

> I am the vine; you are the branches. If a man re-
> mains in me and I in him, he will bear much fruit;
> apart from me you can do nothing *(John 15:5).*

Endurance pays off. There will be a harvest; there will be a trophy for the winner. No true athlete would even consider quitting in the middle of a race. If a hurdle suddenly comes into view (difficulties—or, as a friend of mine calls them, *challenges*), we try to leap over them and continue running.

Most of us are in the middle of our race. We need to be reminded to not lose heart. In the dailiness and monotony of putting one foot in front of the other, it's easy to lose sight of the goal or to forget *why* we are running.

A sudden obstacle may seem too great to overcome. But God has His reasons for those hurdles. There are lessons we need to learn, lessons that not only will strengthen our own spirituality but also, when shared, will help those who follow behind us. The lessons we learn will make the path smoother for others.

> Therefore, strengthen your feeble arms and weak
> knees. "Make level paths for your feet," so that the lame
> may not be disabled, but rather healed *(Heb. 12:12-13).*

In our life of holiness, one of the most important things we can do is to reach out to others and help them run the race also. This isn't a race where we compete against the other runners; it's a race that counts only when we finish the course. Part of the race is making sure the other runners complete their course too. This is considered "running well" (see Gal. 5:7, KJV).

This is holiness in action—reaching out to help others live the holy life too. So many times my telephone rings, and the voice on the other end says, "I'm facing this [hurdle]; what should I do?" Often it's a problem I've run up against myself. The best answer I can give is, "When that happened to me, I learned that God was teaching me this lesson."

It's a great relief to the other person to realize that other people have faced this obstacle and have overcome it.

I've made mistakes, errors in judgment, and poor choices. In each case I've fallen flat on my face in front of the whole watching crowd. But as God has confronted me with those things and has shown me how far they are from His standard of holiness, He has helped me grow and become more discerning.

And, although it would have been better not to have made those wrong choices in the first place, God has used those situations as growing times. He has drawn me closer to Him through His mercy.

As we are becoming holy women, we need to recognize that others are also in the process of becoming holy. If you were there when a Christian sister strayed from God's path, allow God's grace to remove that memory from you. If she has taken care of the problem between herself and God, He has forgiven her and no longer remembers that transgression. You must do the same thing—forget it completely!

Allow her to grow in the Lord. Help her to grow. Growing in God's grace doesn't happen all on its own. We have to nurture the impulse to grow.

> For this reason, since the day we heard about you, we have not stopped praying for you and asking God to fill you with the knowledge of his will through all spiritual wisdom and understanding. And we pray this in

order that you may live a life worthy of the Lord and may please him in every way: bearing fruit in every good work, growing in the knowledge of God *(Col. 1:9-10)*.

Each of us is running a different course. We are not running in duplicate lanes, but we *are* running side by side. The longer we run, the more each of us learns to depend on the Holy Spirit to give us guidance.

I attended a high school girls' cross-country race where several teams were competing. Since many were from out of town, the course laid out for them was on unfamiliar ground. All along the track the coaches had stationed people to point the way to the runners. As each girl approached one of these people, the helper would point to the left or right and call out directions: "Over the hill and turn right," or "between those two trees and down the slope."

This is what the Holy Spirit does for each of us. He knows the way of the path marked "Holiness." It is up to us to listen for His guidance and to be obedient to His directions.

If we trust His guidance, we will complete the race victoriously. God will not call you to run in a situation in which you cannot succeed. This path marked "Holiness" is absolutely possible. It may sound, in the beginning, as if it would be impossible to follow the call to "be holy, because I am holy" (1 Pet. 1:16). But God is trustworthy. Because He calls us to be holy, we can be assured that He makes it *possible* to be holy.

His divine power has given us everything we need for life and godliness through our knowledge of him who called us by his own glory and goodness. Through these he has given us his very great and precious promises, so that through them you may participate in the divine nature and escape the corruption in the world caused by evil desires *(2 Pet. 1:3-4)*.

> Therefore, my brothers, be all the more eager to make your calling and election sure. For if you do these things, you will never fall, and you will receive a rich welcome into the eternal kingdom of our Lord and Savior Jesus Christ *(vv. 10-11)*.

He has given us everything we need to live the holy life. There can be no excuse for disobeying God's command to be holy. Either God can supply *all* that we need, or He can't. And we know that:

> Nothing is impossible with God *(Luke 1:37)*.
>
> Jesus replied, "What is impossible with men is possible with God" *(18:27)*.

If God says it can be done, then we need to seek His way of doing it. One of the ways God helps us springboard over these hurdles is by using **praise.** God, who dwells within us, is many things. He is our Strength, our Shield, our Fortress, our Peace. David, who was called of God to be king over Israel, had to battle his way to the steps of the throne. In Psalm 59, he talks about all the adversaries, the people who were trying to prevent him from reaching the throne. But he ends his list with praise for God.

> But I will sing of your strength, in the morning I will sing of your love; for you are my fortress, my refuge in times of trouble. O my Strength, I sing praise to you; you, O God, are my fortress, my loving God *(vv. 16-17)*.

By praising God in our adversity, we are focusing our eyes on Him rather than on the difficulty. It helps us to remember that God himself, who is pure holiness, is able to keep us holy no matter what is happening around us. When our eyes are focused on Jesus, He imparts His strength to us. He gives us power in our weakness.

> But he said to me, "My grace is sufficient for you, for my power is made perfect in weakness." Therefore I will boast all the more gladly about my weaknesses, so that Christ's power may rest on me. That is why, for Christ's

sake, I delight in weaknesses, in insults, in hardships, in persecutions, in difficulties. For when I am weak, then I am strong *(2 Cor. 12:9-10)*.

But those who hope in the Lord will renew their strength. They will soar on wings like eagles; they will run and not grow weary, they will walk and not be faint *(Isa. 40:31)*.

So do not fear, for I am with you; do not be dismayed, for I am your God. I will strengthen you and help you; I will uphold you with my righteous right hand *(41:10)*.

But you will receive power when the Holy Spirit comes on you; and you will be my witnesses in Jerusalem, and in all Judea and Samaria, and to the ends of the earth *(Acts 1:8)*.

Our running approach to a hurdle is to *praise in adversity.* God then provides *power in our weakness.* The result is *peace in chaos.* We sail over that hurdle through the power of the Holy Spirit. What we thought would devastate us becomes a time of inner peace as we focus on Jesus.

The Lord gives strength to his people; the Lord blesses his people with peace *(Ps. 29:11)*.

Great peace have they who love your law, and nothing can make them stumble *(119:165)*.

You will keep in perfect peace him whose mind is steadfast, because he trusts in you *(Isa. 26:3)*.

If you can remember the three words "praise, power, peace," you'll have a working formula for allowing God's holiness within you to become reality in your everyday life. It is His holiness within us, properly flowing through us, that causes us to run the race victoriously.

Remember, it is how *well* we run the race that counts. Let's run it well. Let's end it triumphantly! Let's praise God constantly. It's the greatest tool the Holy Spirit gives us as we run.

How, then, shall we praise Him? The Bible is filled with

examples of people praising God, but the greatest concentration of praises is found in the Book of Psalms. We can sing praise, whisper it, shout it from the mountaintops or pour it out in prayer.

> Praise the Lord. Praise God in his sanctuary; praise him in his mighty heavens. Praise him for his acts of power; praise him for his surpassing greatness. Praise him with the sounding of the trumpet, praise him with the harp and lyre, praise him with tambourine and dancing, praise him with the strings and flute, praise him with the clash of cymbals, praise him with resounding cymbals. Let everything that has breath praise the Lord. Praise the Lord *(Psalm 150)*.

We have defined our goal in the Christian race as Jesus Christ. Eventually we will come to the place where our race is ended. What happens then? The apostle Paul tells us that there is an everlasting crown for each of us who completes the course.

> Everyone who competes in the games goes into strict training. They do it to get a crown that will not last; but we do it to get a crown that will last forever *(1 Cor. 9:25)*.

I love to watch the Olympic Games on television. My favorite event is ice skating. No matter how difficult and intricate it's been, when the skater finishes her performance, she is rewarded with flowers. Even if she has faltered or fallen, someone always gives her a beautiful bouquet.

If her performance has been particularly wonderful, the audience will throw roses down to her from the grandstands. But no matter how well she has skated, she must wait until she is finished before being showered with roses. If the audience tossed their reward during the performance, the skater would trip and fall with so many flowers on the ice.

There is a reward for us. Someone is waiting with a

crown and a "bouquet of roses." But we have to wait until we've finished the course before we can receive it.

> I have fought the good fight, I have finished the race, I have kept the faith. Now there is in store for me the crown of righteousness, which the Lord, the righteous Judge, will award to me on that day—and not only to me, but also to all who have longed for his appearing *(2 Tim. 4:7-8)*.

Holiness isn't an option in the life of a Christian. It's the only way we can finish the race triumphantly. The watching crowds are cheering us on, just waiting for us to cross the finish line.

Becoming holy women isn't easy. No one ever promised that it would be without difficulties. But the rewards are worth it both here on earth and in heaven to come. Here on earth our lives will take on a quality of richness and luster that was previously lacking. His holiness will permeate our hearts and minds, changing us into pure gold that's been refined by fire. The shine of God's holiness within us will reach out and grace the lives of those around us.

Becoming holy women will produce the heavenly reward of hearing Christ's welcoming voice saying, "Well done!" What crown could be greater than God's approval?

May God richly bless you as you join me on the path marked "holiness." Together we are becoming holy women.

> And a highway will be there; it will be called the Way of Holiness. The unclean will not journey on it; it will be for those who walk in that Way *(Isa. 35:8)*.

* * *

THINK ON THESE THINGS

1. What do you need to get rid of (change) in order to run this race well?

2. What hurdle (challenge or lesson) are you facing right now?

3. What can you do to help a Christian sister grow in the knowledge and grace of our Lord? Name the person and exactly what you plan to do.

4. What excuses are you using to not follow God's command to be holy? What scripture can you find to either substantiate your claim or to repudiate it?

5. In what way can you begin praising God right now as you face the hurdles in your path so that God can give you the strength to "leap over" them?

6. Send a note or card to someone, and tell her that you appreciate the life of Christ shining through her. Let her know you are cheering her on.

7. How has your life changed since you began to put into practice the ideas in this book on *Becoming Holy Women?*

*   *   *

Books to read:

The Ministry of Intercession, F. J. Huegel
Prayer's Deeper Secrets, F. J. Huegel
A Christian's Secret of a Happy Life, Hannah Whitall Smith

Notes

CHAPTER 1:

1. Richard S. Taylor, *Exploring Christian Holiness,* vol. 3, *The Theological Formulation* (Kansas City: Beacon Hill Press of Kansas City, 1985), 179-81.

2. Oswald Chambers, *My Utmost for His Highest* (New York: Dodd, Mead & Co., 1966), 337.

CHAPTER 4:

1. F. J. Huegel, *Prayer's Deeper Secrets* (Minneapolis: Bethany Fellowship, Inc., 1967), 72-74.

2. E. M. Bounds, *Purpose in Prayer* (Chicago: Moody Press, n.d.), 16.